Forming a Limited Company

Forming a Limited Company

10TH EDITION

A practical guide to legal requirements and procedures

Patricia Clayton

Acknowledgement
The forms are Crown copyright and are reproduced with the permission of the Controller of The Stationery Office.

The author acknowledges the kind assistance of Companies House, Cardiff, in the preparation of this book.

First published in Great Britain in 1990
Second edition 1991
Third edition 1992, reprinted with revisions 1993
Fourth edition 1994, reprinted with revisions 1995
Fifth edition 1996
Sixth edition 1998
Seventh edition 2001
Eighth edition 2004
Ninth edition 2006
Tenth edition 2008

120 Pentonville Road
London N1 9JN
United Kingdom
www.koganpage.com

ISBN 978 07494 5304 6

British Library Cataloguing-in-Publication Data

A CIP record for this book is available from the British Library.

Typeset by Jean Cussons Typesetting, Diss, Norfolk
Printed and bound in Great Britain by Bell & Bain Ltd, Glasgow

can you give you the day to day flexibility your business needs, as there is no fixed repayment. However, if your business account remains overdrawn or if you are purchasing larger assets, such as premises, equipment or machinery, it is often better done with structured finance, which means a loan could be a better option. Business loans are usually taken out over a fixed term that can be anything from six months to 25 years, often with the benefit of a fixed interest rate and the security of a structured repayment programme for easy budgeting.

One option is to borrow from family and friends. A clear advantage of this is the flexibility it will give you in your repayments. But if you do go down this route it's essential to put a formal agreement in place, so everyone involved knows where they stand from the start. Borrowing from a relative or a friend, might ease the strain in some senses, but equally it can leave more scope for things to go wrong. Arguments over loans are not uncommon, so to avoid things turning sour, you should not enter into any agreement lightly.

- **Factoring or invoice discounting:** Raising cash against your invoices can be useful if you find that you are having to spend a lot of time chasing late payers or if you are planning a fast period of growth for your company. It's a useful way to release cashflow, while you are waiting for payments. The types of factoring and invoice discounting products available do vary, but it's not unusual for firms to receive up to 90 per cent of the value of their debt book using this form of finance.
- **Leasing/Hire purchase:** Leasing and hire purchase are simple ways to fund the purchase of capital items like cars and computers whose value depreciates over time. Often arrangements and rental payments can be tailored to the income flows of your business and it can make it easier to upgrade to new models. Several types of arrangement are possible and each one has its own tax advantages.
- **Selling shares in the business:** Selling shares to family, friends, employees or other investors such as a business angel is an effective way of raising extra capital although it does mean giving up total ownership of the business. There are positives though as investors may also bring valuable management skills to the business and their contribution in this sense should be one of the key selection criteria. Larger businesses, typically those with a requirement for one million pounds or more and can demonstrate a trading track record are more likely to attract formal venture capital.
- **Grants:** Grants are available from Europe, national government and local authorities and will vary regionally, depending on how you organise your business and the

fiscal year in which you apply. You can get advice on how to apply successfully from your local business link. Most grant providers will be looking for you to show that the grant will assist their policy objectives by, for instance, creating employment in regeneration areas. However, grants can be complex and can take valuable time out from a working day often without results, professional fees may be incurred and often the timescales between application and actually using the money can be long.

Whatever you are looking for, you will only get the attention of a lender or investor if you are able to provide a robust business plan, setting out your idea, objectives, and key business information including financial requirements and projections. The business plan is your chance to demonstrate how the money you are requesting will be used and, if appropriate, how it will be repaid. It's fair to say that the length and complexity of the plan will depend on the amount of funding you are looking for but don't put unnecessary detail into the main body of the plan, as your plan needs to be engaging to potential investors or lenders. The best plans are often relatively short, with more detailed information being put in the appendices.

When you are looking for finance, it is well worth taking advice, before you make any decisions, your banker, accountant or business advisor are a good place to start. Whichever route you choose to finance your business, it's important that you remember the responsibility that comes with borrowing money. Hopefully, you won't encounter too many problems, but if you do experience difficulties or even if you're simply looking for advice you should speak to your bank or investor immediately. As always, the earlier you highlight any potential issues, the better.

For further guidance and practical help on a wide range of business issues visit **www.lloydstsb.com/business**

Where fixed quotations cannot be provided, we will agree with clients a realistic budget for the work to be carried out, before commencing.

Our client services include:

- Advising on patentability of inventions, including novelty investigations;
- Drafting patent specifications, preparing and filing patent applications, and handling all stages of the applications through to grant of patents, in the UK, in Europe and worldwide;
- Assisting in the licensing of intellectual property rights, from preliminary negotiation to the settling of licence agreements;
- Advising on branding, including the freedom to use and registrability of trade marks;
- Handling all stages of the registration of trade marks and designs, in the UK, in Europe and worldwide;
- Patent, design and trade mark opposition and revocation proceedings;
- Patent validity and infringement opinions;
- IPR audits and due diligence investigations.

We offer flexibility in communications – our clients can choose whether to receive documents by paper or electronically. We can even provide alerts by text messaging, if required.

Cost-Effective Protection for Start-ups and Established Companies

We see our job as finding practical solutions for our clients' business needs. If a client's needs are best served by not incurring costs, we will say so. If action is needed, we will help the client decide what is the most cost-effective use of resources. This approach has enabled us to build long-term relationships with successful companies.

persistent breaches of the filing requirements.

Regulations brought in under the new Act bring in a more onerous regime in relation to penalties as from 1 February 2009. The penalties will double if companies default more than once in relation to accounts for financial years beginning after 6 April 2008.

Current filing penalties (until 1 February 2009) – private company

Length of Period	Penalty payable
Not more than 3 months	£100
More than 3 months but not more than 6 months	£250
More than 6 months but not more than 12 months	£500
More than 12 months	£1,000

New filing penalties (as of 1 February 2009) – private company

Length of Period	Penalty payable	Penalty payable if default more than once – accounts for periods beginning on or after 6 April 2008
Not more than 1 month	£150	£300
More than 1 month but not more than 3 months	£375	£750
More than 3 months but not more than 6 months	£750	£1,500
More than 6 months	£1,500	£3,000

Accounts and members

Generally speaking, the annual accounts no longer need to be laid before the members of a private company at a general meeting (normally the Annual General Meeting). Companies still need to ensure that the accounts are circulated to the members. This must be within the timescales laid down under the new Act.

- **Other common filings and returns**

Companies must also make sure that they notify the Registrar in the prescribed form and timescale of other matters affecting a company. The most common of these are the following:

  - Changes to memorandum and articles of association (these documents are the constitution of the company)
  - Change company name
  - Increase share capital
  - Allot new shares
  - Changes in officers – either appointments, resignations, retirements, removals or changes in details
  - Change in accounting reference date (affects the financial year end)

In some cases e.g. change of name, the change will not take effect until the Registrar has confirmed this.

Companies Act 2006

Further changes to date

The following areas (amongst others) have been subject to recent change:

- Prescribed information on websites in relation to company details
- Electronic communications – allowing companies and shareholders to communicate via email, fax, website
- Annual General Meetings – no longer mandatory for new private companies unless required by its constitution or other law
- Accounts – new filing periods
- Meetings and resolutions – changes to procedures to reflect modern business practice, including a new mandatory procedure for written resolutions
- Directors' service agreements
- Inspection of register of members
- Execution of documents.

In October 2008 more changes will be coming in. At Jordans we have made it our business to ensure that we are up to date with the very latest changes in this area. Should you wish to find out more you can subscribe to our email updates by contacting us or visiting our dedicated website at **www.thecompaniesact.co.uk**

* Please note that this article covers changes as at 6 April 2008. This article is a general overview of the requirements affecting private companies. Specific advice would need to be taken depending upon the particular circumstances of your company.

advertisement feature

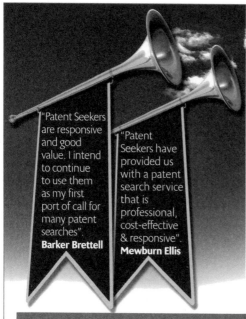

maintenance and installing peripheral drivers are just some of the things that we are regularly asked to help with", David told us. Labyrinth only charges £149.00 per year, per computer for their unlimited Remote Desktop Support service and, in the minority of cases where the problem is not resolved, they locate and task a reputable local company to make an on-site visit at a low fixed fee. Just knowing that there is a friendly, UK based expert to call on when there is a problem gets most companies through the year with no need for an on-site visit.

However, Labyrinth Technology is not just about I.T. support. They are also one of the largest QuickBooks Accounting Software resellers in the UK and, for larger companies or those with more complex requirements, they have recently become solution providers for Interprise, a new, ground breaking package integrating CRM, Accounting, Stock control and E-commerce into one very affordable package.

Labyrinth also supply state of the art VoIP Telephony services from the award winning VoiceNet Solutions platform which allows companies to benefit from a fully featured business telephone system without any of the costs usually associated with telephone switch hardware.

David reminded us, "Technology is meant to make life easier, not be the cause of greater stress. We aim to provide one telephone number for our clients to call for all their technology needs and, when they do call, we take responsibility for their needs and ensure that they are properly supported so they can get on with running their business."

So modern technology may be a maze for many, but there are companies out there that can help guide us!

Contents

Preface

This is a guide for the aspiring entrepreneur starting in business and for those already running a small unincorporated business looking towards expansion. It explains what a private limited liability company is and the protection and advantages of trading with limited liability.

Chapter 1 describes corporate structure and its advantages and explains the procedure for incorporation and registration. Chapter 2 deals with formation and Chapter 3 covers capital structure. Directors' powers and responsibilities are dealt with in Chapter 4, and Chapters 5 and 6 deal with organisation and administration. Since some consideration must be given to what happens if things go wrong, Chapter 7 summarises the repercussions of insolvency, when the real protection given by limited liability comes into its own, and the final chapter sets out the procedure for buying a ready-made 'off the shelf' company. The English version of the forms and documents regulating company life referred to in the text are reproduced in the relevant chapters.

This book is a guide to incorporation of English and Welsh private limited companies but the Companies Acts apply to Scotland with minor adaptations to take into account the requirements of Scottish law. Company legislation in Northern Ireland and Eire has essentially followed the Companies Acts, including changes introduced by EU legislation.

The law stated is at 1st March 2008 and is based on the Companies Acts 1985, 1989 and 2006, the Insolvency Acts 1986 and 2000 and associated legislation, and there are new forms and new fees.

The 2006 Companies Act makes it a lot easier and cheaper to set up and run small private companies.

Relevant changes are noted in the text, but some provisions do not come into force and some forms are not available until October 2009. The Department for

Business, Enterprise and Regulatory Reform (BERR) lists commencement dates and up-to-date information on their website at www.berr.gov.uk, and information is also available on the Companies House website: www.companieshouse.gov.uk.

This book, however, is intended as a guide, not a blueprint for survival, and you are advised to check with Companies House or take expert advice before forming your private limited company and making major decisions about its future.

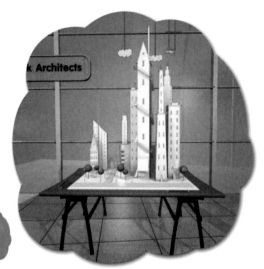

PLANNING YOUR SUCCESS

By Lloyds TSB Commercial

It is often said that if you fail to plan, then you plan to fail and this is certainly the case when it comes to running your own business. Whilst being your own boss can be enjoyable, the lifestyle can be hectic and dealing with day to day issues can push aside the planning that is essential to keep things on the right track.

Preparing and presenting an effective business plan can, therefore, make all the difference between success and failure. Besides being a great way of capturing the long term objectives and financial goals for your business, your business plan can be used to convince prospective lenders, investors and customers that you have thought through your ideas and that they are dealing with a business which has good potential.

Your business plan is also the first step towards making your dreams reality. However, it is not something you just do once at the start of your business, or when you need to raise funds. Rather, a business plan should be seen as a continuously developing document or process. It's a map showing where your business is going and how you are going to get there. It's also a template for action and directs everything you and your people should do to move you towards that goal, although at times you may need to take detours as you can't plan for everything.

A plan should therefore help you in four main ways:

- It gives your business a sense of direction
- It convinces others that you have a well thought through business
- It helps build commitment because you have publicly announced your objectives
- It gives you something to measure your progress against – helping you identify issues early on and take appropriate action

Those who do some business planning are more likely to be successful than those who simply take a more re-active approach and are constantly fire-fighting problems. But planning a business is not a simple matter of scribbling down a few ideas.

Research

Before you start putting a business plan together, it is worthwhile thinking carefully about your business and what makes it tick. Whether you are just starting out or have been up and running for a while, you need to consider what is going to put you ahead of your rivals and how you are going to use your skills and abilities to make a success of the business.

The key to business planning is to think about where you want to go before thinking about how you are going to get there. Similarly, think about how and to whom you are going to sell something before you think about how to provide it. Many businesses fail

advertisement feature

because they do it the wrong way round and concentrate on producing something 'wonderful' without thinking about how they are going to sell it and who is going to buy it.

This should also be a time to undertake some market research. Talk to your customers to understand what they look for when they are buying your product or service. Ask them if there are other products they might buy from you and what might make people who currently buy elsewhere switch to buying from you? You need to keep an eye on competitors at all times; you won't be able to set realistic targets if you don't know what they are up to. Simply getting hold of copies of their marketing literature, or in the case of retailer, going on a 'mystery shopper' expedition could prove useful.

Once you are familiar with both your own business and the market in which you operate you can now start to plan.

Content

There is no set format for a business plan but it should be written in clear, straightforward language and begin by giving some general background details about the business. Make sure every reader knows what the business is called, when it was founded, the purpose of the business, where it is located and if it is already established, what have been its major achievements. So, if you have already built up a customer base to be proud of don't be afraid to shout it from the rooftops.

Likewise, highlight the particular strengths that you and your management team have to offer. Prospective investors in particular are likely to be impressed by evidence of experience of starting up and running successful enterprises. If you have run a business that has not succeeded in the past then it can often be better to be up-front about this. What did you learn from that experience which will help you with this business?

The plan should be used as an opportunity to explain what you are offering and who your customers are. Describe your existing range of products and services and include details of how you intend to develop them in future. If you are thinking of reaching out to new markets, demonstrate how you are going to achieve this and show that you have the right skills to make it work.

Bear in mind that a proper plan has to cover the financial aspects of your business. To satisfy this need, you need to include details of monthly profit and cashflow forecasts for at least the next year and the assumptions which support them. Identify the principal risks which could throw you off course and what you are doing to mitigate these risks.

The plan is a working document and should be regularly reviewed and updated as the business develops as a minimum annually.

Presentation

Whilst your business plan must not become a triumph of style over substance, presentation is important and it does need to look professional. Some of the larger accountancy firms have departments dedicated to helping companies put together business plans, whilst your local Business Link has counsellors who can often offer guidance free of charge.

It is also prudent to bear in mind that a business plan should be flexible enough to satisfy a range of audiences. If you are looking to raise money from venture capitalists, for example, you will need to make sure you clearly articulate how they will realise their investment in the long term. In this case, you might also be able to seek help from corporate finance specialists.

Ultimately, there is nothing quite like writing down your plans to clarify business priorities in your mind and set out a strategy for the future. Armed with a carefully prepared business plan you will be able to approach meetings with bankers, accountants and customers with more confidence than ever before.

Plan of Action

Finally, a good plan leads to an action plan of practical steps to move your business forward. On the basis of the plan, but not necessarily in it, you should be able to say who is going to do what and when. Specific targets should be set, tasks assigned, and deadlines agreed.

A good plan should help you clearly decide the direction for your business and therefore influence every aspect of your business's operations. However, no business plan should be set in stone. You should regularly check your progress against your plan and should review and revise it as the business develops.

Top tips for successful planning

- Be clear in your own mind what you want before attempting to convince others
- Set aside time to think
- Know your business, your customers and your market
- Ask where your business is now
- Consider where you want to go
- Keep your plan short
- Be clear and concise. Avoid jargon
- Be realistic
- Act on your plan
- Review your plan regularly, if you are off track find out why and take action

For further guidance and practical help on a wide range of business issues visit, **www.lloydstsb.com/business**

1

Why a limited company?

Your business structure is crucial to the way you operate: it is the legal framework which determines your share of profits and losses and your responsibilities to business associates, investors, creditors and employees.

Choices

You have three options:

1. operate on your own as a sole trader;
2. join up with partners; or
3. trade as a limited liability company.

Why a limited company?

Incorporating business activities into a company confers life on the business as a 'separate legal entity'. Profits and losses are the company's and it has its own debts and obligations. The business continues despite the resignation, death or bankruptcy of management and shareholders and it offers the ideal vehicle for expansion and the participation of outside investors.

What sort of company?

The overwhelming majority of companies incorporated in this country are private companies limited by shares – private limited liability companies. As at

31 December 2007 more than 2.2 million companies, including public companies, were listed on the Companies Register in England and Wales, with 118,827 listed on the Companies Register in Scotland. In 2007 271,772 new companies were incorporated in England and Wales and 13,864 in Scotland.

The vast majority of registered companies are private companies. At the end of 2007 only 4 per cent of the companies on the Companies Register in England and Wales and less than 1 per cent in Scotland were public companies.

Our law has now come into line with company law in most other European member states and life is a lot easier for small director-controlled family businesses. Private companies cannot offer shares and debentures to the public, but the directors can retain control by restricting transfer of their shares, and concessions have been made in the requirements for filing smaller companies' accounts and reports. Decisions can be made by written resolution with a simple 75 per cent majority vote, there is no longer a restriction on providing financial assistance for the acquisition and purchase of company shares and it is easier to make capital reductions.

Limited liability partnerships (LLPs) – an alternative corporate structure

LLPs, the latest form of corporate business structure, are organised like a partnership, but the partners, called 'members', have limited liability, and the LLP is liable to the full extent of its assets. The members provide the working capital and share profits and the LLP is taxed as a partnership. Disclosure requirements are similar to a company's. The partners have similar duties to directors and the company secretary, including signing and filing annual accounts and putting together the statement of business affairs in insolvency.

Incorporation costs £20 and demand for LLP incorporation has mainly come from existing partnerships, including professional partnerships.

Advantages of trading as a limited company

Although both LLPs and companies have limited liability, a legal existence separate from management and their members and have their names protected by registration at Companies House, there are major advantages in incorporating your business activities in a limited company. These can be summarised as follows:

- It has flexible borrowing powers.
- The company continues despite the death, resignation or bankruptcy of management and members.
- The interests and obligations of management are defined.
- Appointment, retirement or removal of directors is straightforward.
- New shareholders and investors can be easily assimilated.
- Employees can acquire shares.
- Approved company pension schemes usually provide better benefits than those paid under contracts with the self-employed and those in non-pensionable employment. The level of premium that directors can pay is restricted but there is no limit on the overall contributions paid by the company for the directors, although there is a maximum benefit limit imposed by the HMRC Superannuation Fund Office.
- Taxation: sole traders, partners and partnerships pay income tax. Sole traders' and partners' income is taxed as the proprietors' income, regardless of how much profit is retained as working capital, and interest on loans to the business is taxed as their income. Partners are liable personally and jointly for partnership tax, and if a partner dies, the surviving partners are responsible for partnership tax.
- Directors pay income tax and the company pays corporation tax on company profits, and with current rates of tax company profits earned and retained in the business are assessed to corporation tax at lower rates than if income tax were payable on equivalent profits earned by an unincorporated business.

Limited liability

The main and most important advantage of a private company is the protection given by limited liability. The members' – its shareholders' – only liability is for the amount unpaid on their shares. Since many private companies issue shares as fully paid, if things go wrong your only loss is the value of the shares and any loans made to the company.

You can see the advantage if you compare the position of a sole trader with two separate unincorporated businesses and one becomes insolvent. Without Companies Act protection, the solvent business's assets can be claimed by the creditors of the unsuccessful business. With protection, the creditors usually have no claim.

Protection does not, however, extend to fraud, ie knowingly incurring debts the directors have reason to believe the company cannot or will be unlikely to repay. If proved the directors knew or ought to have known the company had no reasonable prospect of avoiding insolvent liquidation, they can face disqualification or imprisonment. If the creditors lose money, the directors and anyone involved in the fraud can be liable and their personal liability can be without limit. (See also 'Fraudulent trading' and 'Wrongful trading' on page 72.)

Protection of the company name

The sole trader or partnership can put their names on the door and start trading, but names are not private property and anyone can use them. Their only real protection is under the trade marks legislation or by taking legal proceedings in a 'passing-off' action for damages to compensate for loss of goodwill.

The choice of both business and company names is restricted. Company names must be registered with the Registrar of Companies and they are protected by registration on the Registrar's Index of Company Names.

Continuity

A company has a legal existence separate from its shareholders. Once formed it has everlasting life. Directors, management and employees can only act as its agent and it is the company itself which owns property and 'signs' contracts. Shares change hands, and management and the workforce may change while the company continues trading. However, the sole trader's business dies with him or her and, in the absence of contrary agreement, a partnership is dissolved on the resignation, bankruptcy or death of a partner. The artificially created company, however, is only killed off by winding up, liquidation, by order of the court or by the Registrar of Companies.

Borrowing and shares

You can increase the company's permanent capital base by a new issue of shares and a company has uniquely flexible borrowing powers.

You can issue preference shares in return for loans and defer repayment to a fixed date, the happening of a specified event or by fixing the rate of dividend. Preference shares do not usually give a right to vote at company meetings. The 'preference' signifies the holder's right to payment of interest or dividend and to preferential repayment of share capital before other classes of shareholders if the company is wound up.

Debentures provide permanent additional capital and can be issued to carry a fixed rate of interest under a fixed or floating charge on some or all of the company's assets. Debenture holders have preference with regard to repayment of capital and payment of interest in a winding up, even if the issue carries no charge on the assets.

Your bank may require the company to be secured by a floating charge. The charge 'floats' on some or all of the company's assets as they exist or change from time to time and is unique to corporate borrowings. It can cover stock in trade, book debts, furniture, equipment and machinery, as well as goodwill and other unspecified assets. Its advantage is that the secured assets can be freely dealt with, mortgaged or sold in the ordinary course of business until the interest or capital is unpaid or there is any other breach of the agreement with the lender. The charge then becomes fixed and the lender can appoint a receiver.

Outside investment

There are tax incentives for outside investors in small unquoted trading companies under the Enterprise Investment, Venture Capital Trust and Corporate Venturing schemes. Here a 'small' company is one with gross assets of up to £15 million immediately before the issue of the shares purchased by the outside investor and £16 million immediately afterwards.

Small companies with a substantial proportion of income from licence fees and royalties are included in the schemes if that income arises from intellectual property and intangible assets which the company has itself created.

You might also consider one of the revenue-approved Enterprise Management Incentive schemes (EMIs). They cover a similar range of businesses, but some trades are excluded and there may be company law and regulatory requirements. You should therefore obtain professional advice.

Your search for outside investment might start with contacting the British Business Angels Association (BBAA), the national trade association that promotes private investment in new and high-growth potential businesses.

Knowledge transfer partnerships

These are partly government funded and enable your business to work with a research organisation, university or college with relevant business expertise to develop new products, services and processes. There are some limits on sectors and the type of project. You can find partners through specialist knowledge transfer partnership consultants.

Enterprise Investment Scheme (EIS)

The scheme only applies to new companies and enables a private outside investor to make a minority investment of between £500 and £400,000 per annum or 30 per cent of the company's share capital and to obtain 20 per cent income tax relief on his or her stake. Relief on up to half the amount invested in the first six months of the year to a maximum of £50,000 can be carried back to the previous tax year. The relief is available only during the first three years of the company's business life, or by a self-employed person starting in business or incorporating business activities during the first three years' trading, and usually the investment must be for a minimum of five years. No capital gains tax is payable on disposal of shares after three years if the initial income tax relief has not been withdrawn. If there is a loss you can choose between income tax or capital gains tax relief. The scheme covers most trading, manufacturing, service, research and development, construction, retail and wholesaling business. There are some exceptions, including financial services, overseas companies and investment and property companies. There is no limit on the amount of share capital that can be issued under the scheme but the details are complicated. If conditions are infringed, tax relief is revoked retrospectively, interest being charged on the relief, which is taxed as a loan from the Treasury; investors should therefore take advice before proceeding.

The Venture Capital Trust Scheme (VCT)

Companies listed on the Stock Exchange under this scheme invest in small higher-risk unquoted trading companies in the same businesses as the Enterprise Investment Scheme. The investor obtains income tax relief at 30 per cent of an investment in new ordinary shares with an annual limit of £100,000. The shares must be retained for at least five years.

The Corporate Venturing Scheme (CVS)

This is another tax incentive scheme to encourage investment in small higher-risk unquoted trading companies. The investor company obtains 20 per cent corporation tax relief on investments in new ordinary shares held for at least three years. Capital gains tax is deferred if the gain is reinvested in another shareholding under the scheme, and relief is also available against income for capital losses net of corporation tax relief on disposals of shares. The investor's maximum stake cannot exceed 30 per cent and individual shareholders in the small company must retain at least 20 per cent of the small company's share capital. Relief for the investor is safeguarded even if the small company goes into liquidation or receivership.

Revenue approved share incentive schemes

Enterprise Management Incentive schemes (EMIs) assist higher-risk companies to recruit and retain skilled employees, investing time and skill to achieve the companies' potential. Share options with a market value of up to £100,000 can be granted to all employees, subject to a total share value of £3 million. The grant is tax-free, and there is no liability for National Insurance contributions (NICs) and no income tax (IT) when the option is exercised. If the shares are sold at a profit, capital gains tax (CGT) may be reduced by tapering relief which usually starts from the date the option was granted.

Share Incentive Plans (SIPs). Here shares must be retained for 5 years and the employer deducts IT and NIC from the price. The employee pays no IT or NICs when the shares are issued but may be liable for CGT if they are sold within 5 years.

You can also give employees up to £3,000 worth of shares as a gift in any tax year. They can be linked to individual or team performance, length of service, level of pay or hours worked. Dividends are not taxable if up to £1,500 of dividends is reinvested in the company in each tax year and the shares are held for at least 3 years.

Save As You Earn (SAYE) schemes are savings-related and must be available to all employees who have been with the company for a specified time. They can invest up to £250 a month from take-home pay and at the end of the savings contract can use the savings to buy shares at a fixed price. Interest and bonuses at the end of the savings scheme are tax free and there is no IT or NICs when the option is exercised. However, there may be a liability for CGT.

Company Share Option Plans (SCOPs) grant options to buy up to £30,000 worth of shares at a fixed price on a fixed date. No IT or NICs are payable on the grant or when the option is exercised, but there may be liability for CGT when the shares are sold. Shareholders with more than 25 per cent of the company's shares in a company controlled by fewer than four people or their directors are excluded.

Retaining control

The sole trader and the sole distributor of a single-member private company run their own show, but in a partnership or company the majority rules the business. Protection of minority shareholders under the Companies Acts, however, is hard to enforce and in practical terms is not very effective. Most transactions can be ratified, even retrospectively, by majority vote of the shareholders. If you hold 75 per cent of the voting shares, and act in good faith and in the interests of the company as a whole, the minority shareholders can only question your decisions if they can prove fraud.

You can form, and change existing companies into, single-member private companies, thus eliminating all possibility of shareholder conflict. As sole shareholder your name and address must be set out in the register of members, together with the date of the change and a statement that the company is a single-member company. The sole member exercises the powers of the general meeting and must minute all decisions. Details of contracts between the sole member and the company must also be minuted. Where decisions are not minuted, the sole member is liable to pay a fine but the decision remains valid.

The 1989 Companies Act provides for the incorporation of partnership companies – companies whose shares are wholly or partly held by their employees – but the legislative framework is not yet in place.

Tax

The sole trader, the partner and the director pay income tax; companies pay corporation tax.

The sole trader and the partners are liable personally to HM Revenue and Customs for tax on their share of business profits. Under the Self-Assessment rules, retiring partners take their tax liability with them, and when partners die, their tax liability passes to their estate. Partners are separately assessed for income tax on their share of profits. The partnership, however, has to complete a Partnership (Tax) Return setting out the partnership's profits and losses for tax purposes, and showing how they were divided between the partners.

Self-Assessment is based on the current tax year instead of the preceding year's income. You can 'self-assess' the company's tax bill but you still have to provide accounts drawn up in accordance with the Companies Acts or computations showing how the figures have been arrived at from the figures in the accounts. Less strict requirements will apply to accounts and audits when the Company Law Reform Act comes into force. Tax on profits is paid nine months after the end of the accounting period and shareholders pay tax on dividends as part of their own liability to income tax.

A director's income is taxed at source under PAYE, and interest on loans to the company and share income are included in taxable earnings. There are certain advantages if his or her salary exceeds £8,500 per annum; the first £30,000 of 'golden handshakes' paid ex gratia or as compensation for loss of office is tax free and redundancy payments can be claimed if the company is wound up.

The company is taxed separately for corporation tax on business profits. Capital gains are taxed at the same rate as income, whether or not they are distributed as income. For 2007/08 the small companies' corporate tax rate is 20 per cent on taxable profits up to £300,000, increasing to 21 per cent in 2008/09 and 22 per cent in 2009/10. The full rate of 30 per cent, reducing to 28 per cent in 2009/10, is charged on profits exceeding £1,500,000, with marginal relief on profits between £300,000 and £1,500,000.

Capital allowances and various tax incentives for investment in small businesses have made this country a corporate tax haven, so advice should be sought to take maximum advantage of the situation.

There are tax concessions if you incorporate your business and sell it to the company as a going concern in exchange for shares. A further concession extends to an Enterprise Investment Scheme investor's first disposal of shares in your company.

Companies pay capital transfer tax, individuals pay inheritance tax and both pay income tax on capital gains. For the most part, unless your business is very small, a director is better off than a sole trader or partner taking out the same share of profits.

company as an insurance policy. In today's litigious and regulation-driven society a limited company could end up saving you from being "wiped out". As a sole trader or partner, when faced with a claim even the shirt on your back could end up going as part of a settlement. As a limited company the claim cannot extend beyond the company's assets in normal circumstances.

When one looks at the complete picture the compelling factor, even in the simplest of scenarios, is very often the peace of mind that the entrepreneur's personal assets and savings are safe from the clutches of creditors and troublemakers. A sole trader or partner is an easy target, a limited company is not.

The second point is that where one has an external investor or co-shareholder in the company it is vital to have a shareholders' agreement in place. In essence this ensures that in the event of a dispute there is a readily available point of reference leading to a pathway for resolution. This is all the more important where the business is bankrolled by a friend or family member. Some more senior family members who are seasoned businesspeople may rely on their previous good fortune of dispute-free experiences but when they are no longer in control the legal landscape can change dramatically.

There are rarely disputes at the outset when the company is formed and everybody is fired up with enthusiasm. Everybody is best of friends but the harsh reality is that greed and ego often create strife and bring down a business, especially where the main worker is not the main investor. External factors such as fashion, consumer or legislative changes may have a serious impact that requires a root and branch rethink of the original business proposition, leading to fundamental disagreements and differences of opinion.

People have short memories and even a few days later may have difficulty recalling what was agreed upon over brandy and cigars at a family meal in the early hours. Consider further what would occur should the investor die leaving a number of heirs as shareholders.

A shareholders' agreement is best prepared by a solicitor and will cover areas such as what to do if a shareholder wants to leave (possibly to start up in competition), whether a dispute is to be arbitrated or heard in court and prevention of minorities from being squeezed out , amongst other things. Each scenario is different so don't try and crib from another business although you may wish to use their model as a point of reference from which to start.

A formal written agreement is also good at making unscrupulous shareholders think twice, and ensures an ongoing commitment from all parties. Even if you decide to remain as a partnership and do not incorporate you should still have a comprehensive written partnership agreement, similar to a shareholders' agreement.

Whatever you decide upon, remember that these areas of paperwork should not be left until later as the nightmare of shattered dreams and relationships is not easily repaired. All too often I have to listen to people's tales of woe as they engage us to perform a salvage operation on their company.

In short – use a limited company and take professional advice.

Formations Direct prides itself on using professional and experienced staff to deliver a personal service that is unrivalled in quality and price, including after-sales support.

Wishing you good luck with your new business!

©Norman Younger BA(Hons) FCCA is managing director of Formations Direct Ltd,company registration agents. He can be contacted via **www.formationsdirect.com** or on **0800 085 45 05**

2

Forming a private limited company

Companies must comply with the rules of corporate organisation and management contained in the Companies Acts. It is simpler and less costly in this country than in any other major commercial centre to incorporate your business activities.

Company registration

The Companies House main offices are in Cardiff and London and there are regional centres in Edinburgh, Leeds, Manchester and Birmingham. They deal with company registrations and the forms and documentation which the company is required to file in accordance with the companies legislation. There is a great deal of information on their website, www.companieshouse.gov.uk. You can obtain notes for guidance and free statutory forms. The customer care department deals with consumer queries on 0870 33 33 636, or via e-mail on enquiries@companieshouse.co.uk. Single forms can be ordered, but there is a limit on the number of forms sent out by post; most statutory forms can be downloaded from their website.

Electronic incorporation via incorporation agents is increasingly popular. The agent guides you through registration and there is less paperwork. You can, however, choose to incorporate your company and file documents electronically yourself; information about the service is available on the Companies House website. WebFiling is fast and easy to use and delivery and security are guaranteed. Most company information is filed free of charge, some other fees are reduced. You can file documents and communicate with shareholders electronically and by e-mail. Electronically filed information about capital and shareholders is noted in Companies House records and updated in the electronic annual returns; paper-filed information is recorded but not updated.

The PROtected Online Filing service (PROOF) protects the company against fraud, and the Companies House Monitor Service within Companies House Direct (CHD) keeps you up to date with statutory filing requirements.

Choosing your company name

Describing your business activities through your choice of name is effective and cheap advertising, but:

- The last word of the company name must be 'Limited' or 'Ltd'. If your registered office is in Wales, the Welsh equivalent 'Cyfyngedig' or 'Cyf' may be used and company documentation must then also state in English that it is a limited company and the information must be displayed at all places where the company carries on business. Charitable or 'quasi-charitable' companies are exempt from this requirement, but a 'quasi-charitable' company must indicate on its documentation that it is a limited company.
- The name must not be the same as or similar to one appearing in the Index of Names kept by the Registrar of Companies.
- Certain 'sensitive' and prohibited words and expressions listed in Appendix 1 cannot be used without the consent of the Secretary of State or relevant government department. For instance, only authorised banks may use a name which might reasonably be understood to indicate they are in the business of banking.
- The name must not imply a connection with the government or a local authority.
- The name must not be offensive, nor must its use constitute a criminal offence.

Application to register the name is made to the Registrar's Cardiff or Edinburgh office. When permission is granted, the name is reserved pending the passing of a special resolution of 75 per cent of the company's shareholders confirming the name. A copy of the resolution must be sent to the Registrar, together with the registration fee. The name is not effective and may not be used until the Registrar issues the Certificate of Incorporation and permission may be withdrawn before it is issued. The directors are personally liable on contracts made on behalf of the company before issue of the Certificate, so you should allow time for the application for conditional approval to be processed as well as for any delay in sending you the Certificate permitting use of the name.

You can search the index of company names at Companies House or on their website free of charge, but it does not show pending applications. If your name is the same as or 'too like' an existing company's, you may be required to change it within 12 months of registration. The time limit is extended to five years if the Secretary of State feels misleading information or undertakings have been given, or assurances given on registration have not been met. He or she can direct a change of name at any time if the name is so misleading as to the nature of the company's activities that it is likely to cause harm to the public.

Electronic incorporation via incorporation agents is increasingly popular. The agent guides you through registration and there is less paperwork. You can incorporate your company and file documents electronically yourself but you must first register as an Electronic Filing Presenter.

Most company information is filed free of charge and some fees are reduced. When the Company Law Reform Act comes into force companies will be able to communicate with shareholders electronically. You can also file documents via e-mail, but this is mainly helpful to big companies that file documents daily or weekly.

Electronically filed information about capital and shareholders is noted in Companies House records and updated in the electronic annual returns. Paper-filed information is recorded but not updated in future annual returns.

The PROtected Online Filing service (PROOF) protects the company against fraud and the Companies House Monitor Service within Companies House Direct (CHD) keeps you up to date with statutory filing requirements. Details of these services are on the Companies House website.

The Consumer Credit Act 1974

Registration of the name does not imply acceptance for the purpose of this legislation. You can find out if the business requires to be licensed under the Act on the Office of Fair Trading's website, www.oft.gov.uk, or by contacting the OFT's licensing branch at Fleetbank House, 206 Salisbury Square, London EC4Y 8JX (tel: 020 721 8608) or 23 Walker Street, Edinburgh EH3 7HX (tel: 0131 220 5930) to check if the name is acceptable to them. Application forms can be downloaded from their website and are also available from your local trading standards department.

Trade marks

Acceptance of your company name does not mean that it can be used as a trade mark. To ensure that you do not infringe anyone's trade mark rights you should search the appropriate class of goods and services at the UK Intellectual Property Office, Central Enquiry Unit, Concept House, Cardiff Road, Newport, South Wales NP10 8QQ (tel: 08459 500 505) or on their website, www.ipo.gov.uk/tm/htm.

Trade mark rights give an automatic right of action against the infringer. Use of an unregistered name may expose you to the risk of a 'passing off' action, though compensation is payable only if the plaintiff can prove that the public has been confused.

The search for a trade mark is technical and you are therefore advised to use a trade mark agent. Details can be found at www.itma.org.uk, www.cipa.org.uk or www.patent.gov.uk.

Trading names

The restrictions on your choice of trading name are set out in Appendix 1. Otherwise almost any name is acceptable provided it is not misleading or, unless you have the consent of the Minister or relevant department, does not imply a connection with the Royal Family, government or local authority, or national or international pre-eminence.

Displaying the company's name

The company's full name in hard copy, electronic or other form must appear on:

- business letters;
- company notices and publications;
- bills of exchange, promissory notes, letters of credit, cheques, endorsements and orders for money and goods;
- invoices and receipts;
- company websites.

Business letters, order forms and websites must also set out the company's:

- place of registration,
- registered number, and
- registered office address to which formal company documents and notices are sent, including legal proceedings.

The name must also be fixed to, or painted on, the outside of the registered office in a prominent position, and at each of the company's offices, factories and places of business.

If the company is registered for VAT, invoices must carry the VAT registration number, the invoice number, date of supply, description of the supply, amount payable excluding VAT, the rate of VAT and the amount, the rate of any cash discount and the customer's name and address.

Documents to be completed

The following documents must be completed and sent to the Registrar electronically or in hard copy so that incorporation and registration can be effected:

- Application for registration of the company;
- Statement of capital and initial shareholdings;
- Statement of proposed officers (Form 10 – see page 28);
- Declaration of compliance with the requirements on application for registration of a company (Form 12 – see page 31).

The **Application for registration** must state:

- *The company's proposed name:* The last word of the name of companies 'trading for profit must be 'limited', 'ltd' or the Welsh equivalent. If the company is to trade in Wales you can file the Memorandum and Articles in Welsh; they can be filed in an official European Union language if accompanied by a certified translation into English and Form 1106. You can check the availability of the name on the index on the Companies House website or by telephone on 0870 33 33 636.
- *That the registered office* is in England and Wales, or in Wales, Scotland or Northern Ireland (London, Cardiff or Edinburgh is also acceptable); this establishes the company's domicile. Unless you can show management and control are elsewhere, the company operates under British law

and pays British tax. The registered office need not be where you carry on business. It is often convenient to use your accountant's or solicitor's address. It is, however, the address to which important and official documents are sent, including service of legal proceedings. It also fixes the tax district dealing with the company's return and tax affairs, except for PAYE, which is usually dealt with locally where wage records are kept.

- *That the liability of the member(s)/shareholder(s) is limited.* This means that if the company is insolvent, the shareholders are liable to creditors for only the amount still owing on their shares; if they are paid for in full, they have no further liability.
- That the company is to be a private company.

The **Statement of capital and initial shareholdings** must state:

- the total number of the company's shares to be taken on formation by the subscriber(s);
- the aggregate nominal value of the shares, and for value for each class of shares;
- details of the rights attached to the shares;
- the total number of shares of that class;
- the aggregate nominal value of shares of that class, the amount to be paid up and the amount (if any) to be unpaid on account of their nominal value or by way of premium;
- the number and nominal value of each share and class of shares to be taken by each subscriber to the Memorandum on formation;
- the amount to be paid up and the amount (if any) unpaid on each share and class of shares on account of their nominal value or by way of premium.

From October 2009 new companies will not have to specify authorised share capital. This will instead be included in the initial statement of capital on incorporation and updated when necessary, for instance when new shares are issued.

The **Statement of proposed officers** must give details of:

- the person or persons who are to be the first director or directors;
- directors must give dates of birth, full name, previous names, occupation, other directorships and addresses for service (for receiving company and legal documents);

Protecting your Assets

(by Jacqueline Needle, Beck Greener)

When Ron Hickman was making his work bench in his garage, and selling it by mail order, he might have thought it too expensive to patent his invention. Fortunately, he did not, and Black & Decker had to pay him licence fees to make and market their famous "Workmate". The patents also enabled Hickman to stop competitors from making and selling their own versions of what has remained a very profitable product.

There are many more examples of innovative products making individuals and companies wealthy not only because of the inherent merits of the products, but also because they were appropriately protected by Intellectual Property Rights (IP).

IP is the collective term for rights such as copyright, trade marks, design rights, registered designs and patents. Whilst all of these rights are important, a new company should pay particular attention to choosing a company name that it is free to use, and which has the potential to become valuable as goodwill attaches to it through that use.

The Registrar of Companies may allow you to register a name for your company, but that does not mean that you are free to use it. For example, Kodak is a very well known trade mark which is registered for many classes of goods and services. Whilst companies such as "Kodaklean Limited" and "Kodak Security Limited" have been registered by Companies House, use of the word Kodak by either company to market their goods and services may infringe those trade mark registrations. Registration of a trade mark gives the trade mark owner the right to prevent others using marks which are identical or similar to the registered trade mark.

advertisement feature

The law of passing-off protects a business against misrepresentations which are likely to damage its goodwill. Therefore, it may still not be possible to use a company name as a trading style, even though the name is not registered as a trade mark. A competitor with rights to the same or a similar name can take action to prevent use of the chosen name, and has a wide range of remedies which include injunctions, damages and an order for repayment of his or her legal costs. In an emergency situation an injunction can be granted quickly to preserve the position pending trial.

It is not a defence that the infringer was not aware of the competitor's prior rights, nor that the company name is registered.

A company which finds itself unable to trade using its chosen company name will have to incur costs changing the name. Stationery, packaging, advertising and promotional material will have to be discarded and replacements printed. All the marketing effort to that point will have been wasted. There may also be legal and related costs because of the dispute with the rights owner. It is far better to get the name choice right from the outset.

Before deciding on a company name, investigate whether proposed names are likely to infringe the rights of others. To avoid incurring professional fees on clear non-starters, an incremental approach can be used. Start with some in-house research using the resources identified below. Remember that the primary objective of the research is to avoid conflict with competitors. If the results look dangerous then move on and choose another name.

When self-checking reveals a favoured name that seems to be clear from potential conflict, seek expert advice from a Trade Mark Attorney who can conduct searches of the UK and other relevant trade mark registers and provide a detailed report as to any risks which might arise from use of that name. Such professional advice is not expensive when compared, for example, to advertising costs, and will be money well spent if it avoids a costly mistake. The Trade Mark Attorney can also recommend the trade mark protection to be sought, and the costs involved.

Of course, company names are only one type of trade mark. The strategy outlined above should also be followed prior to using any trading name, brand, trade mark or logo.

To investigate the marks your competitors use:

- Look at telephone directories and The Yellow Pages.
- Look at trade magazines and journals.
- See if the .co.uk; .com domain names have been registered and if possible visit the websites.
- Put your name of choice into internet search engines.

Then seek advice from a Trade Mark Attorney.

Jacqueline Needle is a Chartered Patent Attorney, a European Patent Attorney, and a Trade Mark Attorney. Jacqueline is also one of the select group of patent attorneys in the United Kingdom with a Litigator's Certificate which gives her the right to conduct litigation in IP matters in all of the English courts. Jacqueline has extensive experience of patent drafting and prosecution both in the United Kingdom and in other countries. She is a partner of Beck Greener in London and can be contacted at:

jneedle@beckgreener.com Tel: **020 7693 5600**

The Beck Greener website: **www.beckgreener.com**

- the secretary or joint secretaries of the company, if any – private companies are not required to have a company secretary after 6 April 2008; they need only give their name, previous name and their residential address or the company's registered office address.

The first director(s) and secretary, if any, must sign and date the form of consent to act. It must also be signed and dated by the subscriber(s) to the Memorandum or by an agent acting on their behalf.

The **Declaration of compliance with the requirements on application for registration of a Company** must be signed and dated by a proposed director or directors or the company secretary (if any) named in Form 10, or by a solicitor dealing with the company's formation. It must be sworn before a Commissioner for Oaths or a Solicitor having the power conferred on a Commissioner for Oaths, or before a Notary Public or Justice of the Peace. They must also state the place where the Statement was sworn, and date the form.

The completed forms must be sent to the Registrar with the registration fee of £20. A same-day service for incorporation and registration costs £80; electronic incorporation costs £15.

It is at this stage that the proposed name is checked. Subject to approval, the Certificate of Incorporation giving the date of signature and registered number of the company is issued. These must be put on all documents sent to the Registrar.

As from the date of issue of the Certificate, the subscribers form a body corporate – the new company – which exercises its own powers. Prior to that date the company has no existence, so any business contracts already agreed are the personal responsibility of the signatories.

The Memorandum of Association

The Memorandum of Association sets out:

- the names of the subscribers;
- that they wish to form a company;
- that they agree to become members/shareholders of the company; and
- that they agree to take at least one share in the company each.

If there are two or more shareholders, at least two of them must sign the Memorandum.

The Articles of Association

The Articles deal with your internal organisation, the company's relationship with shareholders and their relationship with each other, the issue of share capital, powers of directors and proceedings at meetings.

Your new private company can use shortened and simplified Articles under the 2006 Act. Until October 2009, however, you will have to use 'draft model Articles' because the Articles are still under discussion. Finalised Articles will apply to companies incorporated on or after 1 October 2009 which choose to adopt them, and to companies that do not register their own Articles.

The new Articles can be entrenched, that is, they can state that certain Articles can only be amended or altered if specific conditions are met or procedures followed.

Classes of shares

You may want to divide shareholdings into several classes of shares, with different rights attached to each class. The ordinary shares usually carry voting rights and a share of profits (payable as dividend) but shares can be issued carrying increased voting rights or priority in right to dividend or repayment of original capital if the company is wound up. The Articles can set out how rights can be altered or new rights or classes of shares created and, unless they state otherwise, the changes can then be made by a special resolution passed at a general meeting of at least 75 per cent of the holders of that class sanctioning the variation or with the written consent of at least three-quarters in nominal value of the issued shares of that class.

Restrictions on issue of shares

If the company has only one class of shares, the directors have a statutory right under the 2006 Act to issue and take up more shares, grant rights to subscribe for them or issue securities convertible into shares, without first offering them to other shareholders. Their authority to allot shares when there is more than one class of share is dealt with on page 108.

Restriction on share transfers

In order to retain control, directors of private companies usually want to restrict the transfer of shares. They can issue shares with such rights or restrictions as

Companies House
for the record

1106

Voluntary translation of an original filing received by the Registrar after 31/12/2006

(see note 1)

Please complete in ENGLISH in typescript, or in bold black capitals.

CHFP000

Company Number

Company Name in full

Description of filing to which translation relates

Day Month Year

Date the filing was registered at Companies House
(see note 2)

Please indicate the language of the voluntary filing
(see note 3)

Tick box to confirm the voluntary translation is certified ☐
(see note 4)

Signed **Date**

**Delete as appropriate

(** serving director / secretary / administrator /administrative receiver / receiver manager / receiver)

Contact Information
You do not have to give any contact information in the box opposite but if you do, it will help Companies House to contact you if there is a query on the form. The contact information that you give will be visible to searchers of the public record.

Tel

DX number DX exchange

Companies House receipt date barcode

This form has been provided free of charge by Companies House.

For the latest version of this form please visit: www.companieshouse.gov.uk

12/2006

When you have completed and signed the form please send it to the Registrar of Companies at:

Companies House, Crown Way, Cardiff, CF14 3UZ **DX 33050 Cardiff**
for companies registered in England and Wales **or**
Companies House, 37 Castle Terrace, Edinburgh, EH1 2EB **DX 235 Edinburgh**
for companies registered in Scotland **or LP - 4 Edinburgh 2**

Figure 2.1 Statement of voluntary translation of a filing

Companies House
— for the record —

10

Please complete in typescript, or in bold black capitals.
CHWP000
Notes on completion appear on final page

First directors and secretary and intended situation of registered office

Company Name in full

Proposed Registered Office
(PO Box numbers only, are not acceptable)

Post town

County / Region | Postcode

If the memorandum is delivered by an agent for the subscriber(s) of the memorandum mark the box opposite and give the agent's name and address.

Agent's Name

Address

Post town

County / Region | Postcode

Number of continuation sheets attached

You do not have to give any contact information in the box opposite but if you do, it will help Companies House to contact you if there is a query on the form. The contact information that you give will be visible to searchers of the public record.

Tel

DX number | DX exchange

Companies House receipt date barcode
This form is been provided free of charge by Companies House

v 08/02

When you have completed and signed the form please send it to the Registrar of Companies at:
Companies House, Crown Way, Cardiff, CF14 3UZ **DX 33050 Cardiff**
for companies registered in England and Wales
or
Companies House, 37 Castle Terrace, Edinburgh, EH1 2EB
for companies registered in Scotland **DX 235 Edinburgh**

Figure 2.2 Statement of first director(s) and secretary and intended situation of registered office

Company Secretary (see notes 1-5)

Company name

NAME *Style / Title *Honours etc

* Voluntary details

Forename(s)

Surname

Previous forename(s)

Previous surname(s)

Address

Usual residential address
For a corporation, give the registered or principal office address.

Post town

County / Region Postcode

Country

I consent to act as secretary of the company named on page 1

Consent signature **Date**

Directors (see notes 1-5)

Please list directors in alphabetical order

NAME *Style / Title *Honours etc

Forename(s)

Surname

Previous forename(s)

Previous surname(s)

Address

Usual residential address
For a corporation, give the registered or principal office address.

Post town

County / Region Postcode

Country

Day Month Year

Date of birth **Nationality**

Business occupation

Other directorships

I consent to act as director of the company named on page 1

Consent signature **Date**

Figure 2.2 *continued*

Directors (continued) (see notes 1-5)

NAME *Style / Title ____ *Honours etc ____

* Voluntary details

Forename(s) ____

Surname ____

Previous forename(s) ____

Previous surname(s) ____

Address ____

Usual residential address
For a corporation, give the registered or principal office address.

Post town ____

County / Region ____ Postcode ____

Country ____

	Day	Month	Year		
Date of birth				**Nationality**	

Business occupation ____

Other directorships ____

I consent to act as director of the company named on page 1

Consent signature ____ **Date** ____

This section must be signed by
Either

an agent on behalf of all subscribers — **Signed** ____ **Date** ____

***Or* the subscribers**

(i.e those who signed as members on the memorandum of association).

Signed ____ **Date** ____

Signed ____ **Date** ____

Signed ____ **Date** ____

Signed ____ **Date** ____

Signed ____ **Date** ____

Signed ____ **Date** ____

Figure 2.2 *continued*

Companies House
— for the record —

12

Declaration on application for registration

Please complete in typescript, or in bold black capitals.

CHWP000

Company Name in full

I,

of

† Please delete as appropriate.

do solemnly and sincerely declare that I am a † [Solicitor engaged in the formation of the company][person named as director or secretary of the company in the statement delivered to the Registrar under section 10 of the Companies Act 1985] and that all the requirements of the Companies Act 1985 in respect of the registration of the above company and of matters precedent and incidental to it have been complied with.

And I make this solemn Declaration conscientiously believing the same to be true and by virtue of the Statutory Declarations Act 1835.

Declarant's signature

Declared at

Day Month Year

On

➊ Please print name.

before me ➊

Signed **Date**

† A Commissioner for Oaths or Notary Public or Justice of the Peace or Solicitor

Please give the name, address, telephone number and, if available, a DX number and Exchange of the person Companies House should contact if there is any query.

Tel

DX number DX exchange

Companies House receipt date barcode

This form has been provided free of charge by Companies House.

Form revised June 1998

When you have completed and signed the form please send it to the Registrar of Companies at:

Companies House, Crown Way, Cardiff, CF14 3UZ **DX 33050 Cardiff**
for companies registered in England and Wales
or
Companies House, 37 Castle Terrace, Edinburgh, EH1 2EB
for companies registered in Scotland **DX 235 Edinburgh**

Figure 2.3 A declaration of compliance with the requirements on application for the registration of a company

the shareholders decide by ordinary majority resolution, and the draft model Articles permit them to refuse to register transfers of shares which are not fully paid or on which the company has a lien, without prejudice to any rights attached to the existing shares.

The directors can also refuse to register transfers unless the share or shares are accompanied by the relevant Share Certificate or other evidence of ownership, or unless the transfer relates to only one class of shares, and owned by not more than four shareholders.

Notice of refusal to transfer must be sent to the shareholder(s) within two months after the date on which the shares were lodged with the company, and the directors can suspend registration of share transfers for up to 30 days in each year.

Purchase by the company of its own shares

Under the draft model Articles private companies can buy their own shares, provided the finance comes out of distributable profits, that is, profits available for payment of dividends, the proceeds of a fresh issue of shares or capital. When the buy back is completed, the relevant shares are automatically cancelled.

You are, however, advised to take professional advice before you take action.

Transmission of shares

The survivor and personal representatives of deceased shareholders, the survivor or survivors of joint shareholders and the personal representatives of a deceased sole shareholder have title to the deceased person's shares, subject to payment of any liabilities attached to the shares.

The person entitled to shares on the death or bankruptcy of a shareholder must notify the company that they have title to the shares; they can instead nominate someone else to be registered as transferee, in which case they must execute an instrument of transfer. Anyone entitled to shares in consequence of the death or bankruptcy of a shareholder has the same rights as other shareholders, except that they cannot attend or vote at company meetings until registered as a shareholder.

Directors

First directors are named in the statement filed on registration and a private company may operate with one director, who cannot also be the company secretary.

Currently anyone can be a director of a private company, provided that he or she is not a bankrupt or disqualified from acting as a director. In Scotland the Registrar will not register a director under 16. The same applies to companies registered in England and Wales as from 1 October 2009, and acting directors under 16 will also be disqualified. Some foreign nationals cannot be directors and you should check with the Border and Immigration Agency, Lunar House, 40 Wellesley Road, Croydon CR9 2BY (tel: 0845 010 5200) or check the website www.ind.homeoffice.gov.uk before appointing a non-British director. The draft model Articles disqualify anyone who is of unsound mind or who is absent from board meetings for more than six months without consent. A company can be a director of another company; directors need not hold shares but the Articles can provide that they be required to do so.

Directors can be apointed and removed by ordinary majority resolution of the shareholders. The resolution overrides any service agreement made between the director and the company, although the director can claim compensation for loss of office on breach of the agreement. The director's position can be safeguarded by giving him or her sufficient special voting rights on shares owned to outweigh the votes of other shareholders.

Directors' powers

Directors run the company on behalf of the shareholders. Directors usually exercise their powers through resolutions passed at board meetings. In larger companies the board deals with general policy; day-to-day decisions are left to the managing director and committees of directors. The smaller company works in the same way but in practice decisions are often made by all the directors on a daily basis.

Directors manage the business. They can exercise all the powers of the company to borrow, mortgage company property and issue securities. You can, however, add a provision which limits the total debt the directors can raise without the shareholders' prior consent.

Directors' salaries

Directors' remuneration and their expenses must be authorised by an appropriate provision in the Articles. Table A provides for payment of such remuneration as the company may by ordinary resolution determine, and payment of travelling, hotel and other expenses properly incurred in connection with attendance at directors' and company meetings and the discharge of their duties. Directors are advised also to agree a full service contract with the company, covering salary, share of profits and/or bonuses and reimbursement of expenses to safeguard their position.

General provisions

The draft model Articles also cover:

- the company's lien on shares for the balance unpaid;
- making calls on shareholders for moneys payable on shares;
- forfeiture of shares where calls have not been paid;
- meetings, notice of meetings and procedure at meetings, including voting procedure; keeping of minutes; declaration and payment of dividends;
- winding up; indemnity of directors and use of the company seal (see page 94).

Duties and fees payable

A fee of £20 is payable to the Registrar of Companies when lodging documents on formation and the fee stamp is affixed on the Memorandum of Association, £50 for same-day incorporation. If you have suitable software, electronic incorporation costs £15 and same-day electronic incorporation £30.

Incorporation

The company exists from the date that the Companies Registration Office issues the Certificate of Incorporation, which is numbered, dated and signed. The name can be changed after incorporation for £10 but not the registered number, so if you want to trace a company you should quote the number.

Companies House
— for the record —

88(3)
(Revised 2005)

Please complete in typescript, or in bold black capitals.
CHWP000

Particulars of a contract relating to shares allotted as fully or partly paid up otherwise than in cash

Note: This form is only for use where the contract has not been reduced to writing

Company Number

Company name in full

gives the following particulars of a contract which has not been reduced to writing

1	Class of Shares (ordinary or preference etc)			
2	The number of shares allotted as fully or partly paid up otherwise than in cash			
3	The nominal value of each such share			
4a	The amount of such nominal value to be considered as paid up on each share otherwise than in cash			
b	The value of each share allotted ie. the nominal value and any premium			
c	The amount to be considered as paid up in respect of b			

continue overleaf

Signed Date

**Delete as appropriate

** A director / secretary / administrator / administrative receiver / receiver / official receiver / receiver manager / voluntary arrangement supervisor

Contact Details
You do not have to give any contact information in the box opposite but if you do, it will help Companies House to contact you if there is a query on the form. The contact information that you give will be visible to searchers of the public record.

Tel

DX number DX exchange

Companies House receipt date barcode

This form has been provided free of charge by Companies House.

08/2005

When you have completed and signed the form please send it to the Registrar of Companies at:
Companies House, Crown Way, Cardiff, CF14 3UZ DX 33050 Cardiff
for companies registered in England and Wales or
Companies House, 37 Castle Terrace, Edinburgh, EH1 2EB DX 235 Edinburgh
for companies registered in Scotland or LP - 4 Edinburgh 2

Figure 2.4 Particulars of a contract relating to shares allotted as fully or partly paid up otherwise than in cash

5 If the consideration for the allotment of such shares is services, or any consideration other than that mentioned in 6,7 or 8 below, state the nature and amount of such consideration, and the number of shares allotted

6 If the allotment is a bonus issue, state the amount of reserves capitalised in respect of this issue

7 If the allotment is made in consideration of the release of a debt, e.g., a director's loan account, state the amount released

8 If the allotment is made in connection with the conversion of loan stock, state the amount of stock converted in respect of this issue

Figure 2.4 *continued*

Pre-incorporation contracts

You can contract for the benefit of your not-yet-incorporated company, but the company must be specifically identified in the contract by name or description. On incorporation, the company has the same rights and remedies under the contract as if it had been a party to the contract.

If, however, you are still at the organising stage, you may prefer to contract on your own behalf as promoter of the still-to-be-incorporated company. You are then personally liable until the contract and should therefore contract on the basis that you will cease to be liable once the contract is put before the board or general meeting on incorporation, whether or not the company adopts the transaction. Once it is adopted, the contract is replaced by a draft agreement, which is executed by the company after incorporation.

Transfer of existing business to your company

You can sell your business to the company for shares issued at par (face value). Assets and liabilities are taken over by the company and no capital gains tax is chargeable provided the only payment is the issue of shares.

A formal transfer agreement should be executed transferring existing assets and liabilities to the company on incorporation, but professional advice should be sought as to the tax and legal aspects of transfer. It is advisable to provide a proper valuation of the assets transferred, although you are not obliged to do so. You should formally disclose details of the transactions to shareholders even if this is a formality at this early stage when the company may have only one or two shareholders. Full details should be put on file and the sale should be properly minuted when the transaction is adopted at the first general meeting.

The sale agreement or prescribed form of details of the sale and Form 88(3) – see page 35 – must be lodged with the Registrar within one month of the transaction. A stamp duty of 15 per cent ad valorem (according to value) is payable on transfer of some assets, including goodwill, unless derived from intellectual property, for instance a trademark, and some debts. There is no charge to duty if the total consideration does not exceed £60,000 and the agreement contains a Certificate of Value, which certifies that 'the transaction hereby effected does not form part of a larger transaction or a series of transactions in respect of which the amount or value or aggregate amount or value of the consideration exceeds £60,000'.

Duty of 1 per cent applies to transactions between £125,001 and £250,000, 3 per cent to transactions between £250,001 and £500,000 and 4 per cent to transactions over £500,000. The Certificate must state the transaction is within the relevant limits, though no Certificate of Value is required for transactions over £500,000. Stamp duty of 0.5 per cent is payable on the purchase of stocks and shares.

3

Capital

The limited liability company is structured for expansion. Once incorporated, your business easily assimilates additional participants and capital and you can retain control as the majority shareholder.

Corporate capital

The company can build up a complicated capital structure and a whole range of special terms describes capital contributions.

You no longer need to have authorised share capital and there are no restrictions on giving financial assistance to actual and potential shareholders acquiring or purchasing company shares or reducing the company's capital.

Initial capital contributions

When two directors each contribute £400 to form a company with a nominal or authorised capital of £1,000, each taking 500 shares with a par or nominal value of £1 each, that £800 is the company's paid-up capital for 1,000 shares in the company. The balance of £200 outstanding is the uncalled capital. This can be called on by the company at any time, in accordance with the terms of the Articles, unless it is later decided (by special resolution) to make all or part of it reserve capital which is only called on if the company goes into liquidation.

Nominal capital is the total amount of share capital which the Memorandum authorises the company to issue and any reference to capital on business documents must refer to the issued paid-up capital.

Shares

- *Ordinary shares* give you a claim to income on equal parts of the company's net assets.
- *Preference shares* give preferential rights to dividend which must be met before the ordinary share dividend. If *convertible* they carry the option at some stage to convert them into ordinary shares. *Participating preference shares* give a right to participate in, or receive, additional dividend, usually in proportion to the ordinary declared dividend. If dividends cannot be paid to cumulative preference shareholders, they are carried forward to successive years.

  Form 88(2), 128(1), 128(3) or 128 (4) must be sent to the Registrar, depending on whether the shares are given rights that are not contained in the Articles, by amending the Articles or under a resolution or agreement.
- *Redeemable shares* come with an agreement that the company will buy them back after a certain period or fixed date at the option of the company or the shareholder. If not redeemed in accordance with the agreement – eg if redeemed at an earlier date – the transaction amounts to a purchase of the company's shares and Notice of Redemption must be sent to the Registrar within one month on Form 122. The issue may require an alteration to the Articles.
- *Partly paid up shares and bonus or 'scrip' shares.* Undistributed profits and monies in the 'share premium account' or 'capital redemption reserve' can be used to pay amounts unpaid on shares, or for an issue of wholly or partly paid up bonus shares.
- *Bonus shares* must be allotted to shareholders in proportion to their existing holdings; they do not pay for the shares which are effectively a capitalisation of profits or reserves and stamp duty is not payable.
- *Share warrants* are documents which state that the bearer is entitled to shares. If authorised by the Articles, a company can convert fully paid shares to share warrants, which are easily transferable and can be passed from hand to hand without a transfer document. Vouchers are usually issued with warrants so dividends may be claimed. When issued, the shareholder's name must be deleted from the Register of Members and the date of issue of the warrant and the number of shares to which it relates must be noted. The holder remains a shareholder, but whether they are a member of the company depends on the company's Articles. Subject to the Articles, a share warrant can be surrendered for cancellation, when the holder is entitled to be re-entered into the Register of Members.

Increasing the company's capital

Under the draft model Articles you can increase the company's capital by issuing more shares, agreed by ordinary majority resolution. The new capital can be by issue of ordinary or deferred shares, paid for on instalment terms.

Notice of the increase must be sent to the Registrar with the appropriate form (see above) within 15 days of the passing of the resolution, together with a copy of the Minutes of the Meeting, the authorising resolution and, if required, the printed amended Article.

Directors' authority to allot shares

If the company has only one class of shares, the 2006 Act authorises the directors to issue and take up more shares of the same class, grant rights to subscribe for them or issue securities convertible into shares, without first offering them to the other shareholders. The directors' authority to allot shares when there is more than one class of share is dealt with on page 108.

If the directors hold 75 per cent of the shares with voting rights, the company can be given a wide capital base and they can retain control. Once rights are attached to shares, they can only be varied with the consent of the shareholders affected, however small the group.

The share premium account

If you are trading profitably and have built up reserves, the true value of shares is increased. If new shares are issued at more than the par (nominal) value of previously issued shares of the same class, the premium must be transferred to a share premium account, which becomes part of the company's capital. This can only be used to write off the expenses of another issue, plus any commission paid on the issue of the shares, or for new fully paid up bonus shares.

Reducing the company's capital

You can reduce the company's capital by buying back its shares, provided the finance comes out of distributable profits, that is, profits available for payment of dividends, the proceeds of a fresh issue of shares or capital. When the buy back is completed, the relevant shares are automatically cancelled.

Buy-back is effectively a cash distribution to shareholders. This can of course be done by way of dividend, which attracts stamp duty. With buy-back, however, you can maintain or increase earnings or net assets per share and the selling shareholder may be able to obtain CGT relief. Buy-back also enables current shareholders to retain control.

The company's share capital can also be decreased by passing an ordinary resolution cancelling shares which have not been, or agreed to be, taken up. Notice of the cancellation on Form 122 must be sent to the Registrar within one month.

Company borrowings: mortgages, charges and debentures

Borrowing

There is no restriction on the directors' or the company's borrowing powers.

Mortgages

A money-lending company can lodge its own shares as security in a transaction entered into by the company in the ordinary course of its business and mortgage partly paid-up shares for the balance remaining unpaid.

Debentures

You can raise additional capital by a debenture issue. The debenture itself is a document given by the company to the debenture holder as evidence of a mortgage or charge on company assets for a loan with interest. The holder is a creditor of the company, but often holds one of a series of debentures with similar rights attached to them or is one of a class of debenture holders whose security is transferable (like shares) or negotiable (like warrants).

Fixed charges and floating charges

If the debenture is secured by specific assets, the charge is fixed. A charge over all the company's assets – which will include stock in trade, goodwill and so on – is a floating charge, as the security changes from time to time. A floating charge, which allows the company freely to deal with business assets, automatically crystallises into a fixed charge if the company is wound up or stops trading, or if it is in default under the terms of the loan and the debenture holder takes steps to enforce the security.

You can create separate fixed and floating charges. The floating charge is always enforceable after a fixed charge, in whatever order they were made, unless it prohibits a loan with prior rights on the security of the fixed assets and the lender under the fixed charge knows of the restriction. Banks usually include this provision in their lending agreements covering the company's overdraft, so that you may have difficulties if you run into a basic liquidity problem, as cheques paid into the account after a company ceases trading may be fraudulent preferences.

Registration of charges

All charges, which include mortgages, created by the company must be registered with the Registrar within 21 days of creation. The fee on registration is £13 and £50 for same-day registration. Your bank's charge on credit balances is not registrable unless it is charged to a third party.

If the company charges property, or the charge is created, outside the UK, the 21-day deadline can be extended by application to the Registrar before the filing deadline. The extension runs from the date when the instrument creating the charge could have been received in the UK in the normal course of business.

The requirement covers charges made as security for debentures, floating charges on the company's assets, including a charge on book debts, and charges on any interest in land or goods (except, in the case of goods where the lender is entitled to possession of the goods or of a document of title to them). It also covers charges on intangible moveable property (in Scotland, incorporeal moveable property) such as goodwill, intellectual property, book debts and uncalled share capital or calls made but not paid. Form 395 (see page 45) is used in registering a mortgage or charge and Form 397 (see page 47) for an issue of secured debentures. Unless registered, the charge is void as against the liquidator and any creditor so far as any security on the company's assets is conferred under the charge and the moneys secured are immediately repayable. If the company does not register the charge, the lender or some other interested person can do so.

If incorrect particulars are registered, the charge is void to the extent of the irregularity unless the court orders otherwise but the Registrar will allow a late amendment to the registered particulars. The company and its officers who are in default in registering the instruments are, in addition, liable to a fine of £200 a day until registration is effected. The holder of the unregistered charge is in the position of an unsecured creditor.

Unless the charge was created after the issue, a copy of the certificate of registration issued by the Registrar must be endorsed on every debenture or certificate of debenture stock issued by the company. Free certified copies can be obtained from Companies House.

Copies of every instrument creating a charge which requires registration must be kept at the registered office but it is only necessary to provide a copy of one of a series of uniform debentures.

Charges on registered land must also be registered under the Land Registration Act 2002, and fixed charges on unregistered land registered under the Land Charges Act 1972. You should check with the Land Registry as to requirements.

When a registered charge is repaid or satisfied, a 'memorandum of satisfaction' on Form 403b (see page 177) should be filed with the Registrar.

The Consumer Credit Act 1974

Loans for up to £25,000 including the cost of the credit, where the company is a joint debtor with an individual, must comply with the terms of the Consumer Credit Act 1974. A joint and several obligation by the company and an individual is outside the ambit of the Act.

M

COMPANIES FORM No. 395

395

Particulars of a mortgage or charge

CHWP000

A fee of £13 is payable to Companies House in respect of each register entry for a mortgage or charge.

Please do not write in this margin

Pursuant to section 395 of the Companies Act 1985

Please complete legibly, preferably in black type, or bold block lettering

To the Registrar of Companies
(Address overleaf - Note 6)

For official use

Company number

Name of company

* insert full name of Company

*

Date of creation of the charge

Description of the instrument (if any) creating or evidencing the charge (note 2)

Amount secured by the mortgage or charge

Names and addresses of the mortgagees or persons entitled to the charge

Postcode

Presenter's name address and reference (if any) :

For official Use (02/06)
Mortgage Section

Post room

Time critical reference

Page 1

Figure 3.1 Particulars of a charge

Short particulars of all the property mortgaged or charged

Please do not write in this margin

Please complete legibly, preferably in black type, or bold block lettering

Particulars as to commission allowance or discount (note 3)

A fee is payable to Companies House in respect of each register entry for a mortgage or charge. (See Note 5)

Signed Date

On behalf of [company][mortgagee/chargee]†

† delete as appropriate

Notes

1 The original instrument (if any) creating or evidencing the charge, together with these prescribed particulars correctly completed must be delivered to the Registrar of Companies within 21 days after the date of creation of the charge (section 395). If the property is situated and the charge was created outside the United Kingdom delivery to the Registrar must be effected within 21 days after the date on which the instrument could in due course of post, and if dispatched with due diligence, have been received in the United Kingdom (section 398). A copy of the instrument creating the charge will be accepted where the property charged is situated and the charge was created outside the United Kingdom (section 398) and in such cases the copy must be verified to be a correct copy either by the company or by the person who has delivered or sent the copy to the registrar. The verification must be signed by or on behalf of the person giving the verification and where this is given by a body corporate it must be signed by an officer of that body. A verified copy will also be accepted where section 398(4) applies (property situate in Scotland or Northern Ireland) and Form No. 398 is submitted.

2 A description of the instrument, eg "Trust Deed", "Debenture", "Mortgage", or "Legal charge", etc, as the case may be, should be given.

3 In this section there should be inserted the amount or rate per cent. of the commission, allowance or discount (if any) paid or made either directly or indirectly by the company to any person in consideration of his:
(a) subscribing or agreeing to subscribe, whether absolutely or conditionally, or
(b) procuring or agreeing to procure subscriptions, whether absolute or conditional,
for any of the debentures included in this return. The rate of interest payable under the terms of the debentures should not be entered.

4 If any of the spaces in this form provide insufficient space the particulars must be entered on the prescribed continuation sheet.

5 A fee of £13 is payable to Companies House in respect of each register entry for a mortgage or charge. Cheques and Postal Orders are to be made payable to **Companies House**.

6 The address of the Registrar of Companies is: Companies House, Crown Way, Cardiff CF14 3UZ

Page 2

Figure 3.1 *continued*

M

COMPANIES FORM No. 397

397

Particulars for the registration of a charge to secure a series of debentures

CHFP000

A fee of £13 is payable to Companies House in respect of each register entry for a mortgage or charge.

Please do not write in this margin

Pursuant to section 397 of the Companies Act 1985

Please complete legibly, preferably in black type, or bold block lettering

To the Registrar of Companies
(Address overleaf - Note 7)

For official use

Company number

Name of company

* insert full name of Company

*

Date of the covering deed (if any) (note 2) ______

Total amount secured by the whole series ______

Date of present issue ______

Amount of present issue (if any) of debentures of the series ______

Date of resolutions authorising the issue of the series ______

Names of the trustees (if any) for the debenture holders

General description of the property charged

Continue overleaf as necessary

Presenter's name address and reference (if any) :

For official Use (02/06)
Mortgage Section

Post room

Time critical reference

Page 1

Figure 3.2 Particulars for the registration of a charge to secure a series of debentures

General description of the property charged (continued)

Please do not write in this margin

Please complete legibly, preferably in black type, or bold block lettering

Particulars as to commission, allowance or discount (note 3)

A fee is payable to Companies House in respect of each register entry for a mortgage or charge. (See Note 6)

Signed ______________________ Date ______________

On behalf of [company] [mortgagee / chargee]†

† delete as appropriate

Notes

1 Particulars should be given on this form of a series of debentures containing (or giving by reference to any other instrument) any charge to the benefit of which the debenture holders of the series are entitled pari passu. This form is to be used for registration of particulars of the entire series, and may also be used when an issue of debentures is made at the same time as the series of debentures is created. All issues of debentures made after the registration of the series with the Registrar of Companies should be notified to the Registrar on Form No. 397a.

2 The date should be given of the covering deed (if any) by which the security is created or defined.

3 In this section there should be inserted the amount or rate per cent of the commission, allowance or discount (if any) paid or made either directly or indirectly by the company to any person in consideration of his
(a) subscribing or agreeing to subscribe, whether absolutely or conditionally, or
(b) procuring or agreeing to procure subscriptions, whether absolute or conditional,
for any of the debentures included in this return. The rate of interest payable under the terms of the debentures should not be entered.

4 The deed (if any) containing the charge must be delivered with these particulars correctly completed, to the Registrar within 21 days after it's execution. If there is no such deed, one of the debentures must be so delivered within 21 days after the execution of any debenture of the series.

5 If the spaces in this form are insufficient, the particulars may be continued on a separate sheet.

6 A fee of £13 is payable to Companies House in respect of each register entry for a mortgage or charge. Cheques and Postal Orders are to be made payable to **Companies House**.

7 The address of the Registrar of Companies is: Mortgage Section, PO Box 716, Companies House Crown Way, Cardiff CF14 3YA

Page 2

Figure 3.2 *continued*

M

CHWP000

COMPANIES FORM No. 398

Certificate of registration in Scotland or Northern Ireland of a charge comprising property situate there

398

Pursuant to section 398(4) of the Companies Act 1985

Please do not write in this margin

Please complete legibly, preferably in black type, or bold block lettering

To the Registrar of Companies
(Address overleaf)

For official use

Company number

Name of company

* insert full name of company

*

I ______________________________

of ______________________________

* give date and parties to charge

certify that the charge * ______________________________

of which a true copy is annexed to this form was presented for registration on ______________

† delete as appropriate

in [Scotland] [Northern Ireland] †

Signed

Date

Presenter's name address and reference (if any) :

For official Use (02/06)
Mortgage Section

Post room

Figure 3.3 Certificate of registration in Scotland or Northern Ireland of a charge comprising property situated there

Notes

The address of the Registrar of Companies is :-

Companies House
Crown Way
Cardiff
CF14 3UZ

Figure 3.3 *continued*

M

COMPANIES FORM No. 400

Particulars of a mortgage or charge subject to which property has been acquired

400

CHWP000

A fee of £13 is payable to Companies House in respect of each register entry for a mortgage or charge.

Please do not write in this margin

Pursuant to section 400 of the Companies Act 1985

Please complete legibly, preferably in black type, or bold block lettering

To the Registrar of Companies
(Address overleaf - Note 4)

For official use

Company number

Name of company

* insert full name of Company

*

Date and description of the instrument (if any) creating or evidencing the mortgage or charge (note 1)

Amount secured by the mortgage or charge ____________________

Names and addresses of the mortgagees or persons entitled to the mortgage or charge

Short particulars of the property mortgaged or charged

Continue overleaf as necessary

Presenter's name address and reference (if any) :

For official Use (02/06)
Mortgage Section

Post room

Time critical reference

Page 1

Figure 3.4 Particulars of a mortgage or charge subject to which property has been acquired

Short particulars of the property mortgaged or charged (continued)

Please do not write in this margin

Please complete legibly, preferably in black type, or bold block lettering

Date of the acquisition of the property ______________________________

Signed ______________________ Designation ‡______________ Date ______________

A fee is payable to Companies House in respect of each register entry for a mortgage or charge. (See Note 3)

‡ Insert Director, Secretary, Administrator, or Administrative Receiver as appropriate

Notes

1 A description of the instrument, eg, "Trust Deed", "Debenture", etc, as the case may be, should be given.

2 A verified copy of the instrument must be delivered with these particulars correctly completed to the Registrar of Companies within 21 days after the date of the completion of the acquisition of the property which is subject to the charge. The copy must be verified to be a correct copy either by the company or by the person who has delivered or sent the copy to the registrar. The verification must be signed by or on behalf of the person giving the verification and where this is given by a body corporate it must be signed by an officer of that body. If the property is situated and the charge was created outside Great Britain, they must be delivered within 21 days after the date on which the copy of the instrument could in due course of post, and if despatched with due diligence have been received in the United Kingdom.

3 A fee of £13 is payable to Companies House in respect of each register entry for a mortgage or charge.

Cheques and Postal Orders are to be made payable to **Companies House.**

4 The address of the Registrar of Companies is:-

Companies House
Crown Way
Cardiff
CF14 3UZ

Page 2

Figure 3.4 *continued*

M

COMPANIES FORM No. 410(Scot)

Particulars of a charge created by a company registered in Scotland

410

CHWP000

A fee of £13 is payable to Companies House in respect of each register entry for a mortgage or charge

Please do not write in this margin

Pursuant to section 410 of the Companies Act 1985

Please complete legibly, preferably in black type, or bold block lettering

To the Registrar of Companies (Address overleaf - Note 6)

For official use

Company number

Name of company

* insert full name of company

*

Date of creation of the charge (note 1)

Description of the instrument (if any) creating or evidencing the charge (note 1)

Amount secured by the charge

If there is not enough space on this form you may use the prescribed continuation sheet 410cs

Names and addresses of the persons entitled to the charge

Presenter's name address telephone number and reference (if any):

For official use (02/06)

Charges Section

Post room

Page 1

Figure 3.5 Particulars of a charge created by a company registered in Scotland

Short particulars of all the property charged.

Please do not write in this margin

Please complete legibly, preferably in black type, or bold block lettering

If there is not enough space on this form you may use the prescribed continuation sheet 410cs

Statement, in the case of a floating charge, as to any restrictions on power to grant further securities and any ranking provision (note 2)

Particulars as to commission, allowance or discount paid (see section 413(3))

A fee is payable to Companies House in respect of each register entry for a mortgage or charge. (See Note 5)

Signed ______________________________ Date ______________________

On behalf of [company] [chargee]†

† delete as appropriate

Notes

1. A description of the instrument e.g. "Standard Security" "Floating Charge" etc, should be given. For the date of creation of a charge see section 410(5) of the Act. (Examples - date of signing of an Instrument of Charge; date of recording / registration of a Standard Security; date of intimation of an Assignation.)

2. In the case of a floating charge a statement should be given of (1) the restrictions, if any, on the power of the company to grant further securities ranking in priority to, or pari passu with the floating charge; and / or (2) the provisions, if any, regulating the order in which the floating charge shall rank with any other subsisting or future floating charges or fixed securities over the property which is the subject of the floating charge or any part of it.

3. A certified copy of the instrument, if any, creating or evidencing the charge, together with this form with the prescribed particulars correctly completed must be delivered to the Registrar of Companies within 21 days after the date of the creation of the charge. In the case of a charge created out of the United Kingdom comprising property situated outside the U.K., within 21 days after the date on which the copy of the instrument creating it could, in due course of post, and if despatched with due diligence, have been received in the U.K. Certified copies of any other documents relevant to the charge should also be delivered.

4. A certified copy must be signed by or on behalf of the person giving the certification and where this is a body corporate it must be signed by an officer of that body.

5. A fee of £13 is payable to Companies House in respect of each register entry for a mortgage or charge. Cheques and Postal Orders are to be made payable to **Companies House**.

6. The address of the Registrar of Companies is: Companies House, 37 Castle Terrace, Edinburgh EH1 2EB
DX 235 Edinburgh or LP - 4 Edinburgh 2

Page 2

Figure 3.5 *continued*

4

Directors

The private limited company must have at least one director, although he or she cannot also be the company secretary.

Who is a director?

Anyone, with whatever title and however appointed, who acts as a director, is regarded as a director.

Who can be a director?

Anyone can be appointed as director unless disqualified by the Articles except for:

- an undischarged bankrupt, unless his or her appointment is approved by the court;
- someone disqualified by court order;
- the company's auditor.

The draft model Articles disqualify anyone who is of unsound mind or who is absent from board meetings for more than six months without consent. A company can be your corporate director, and directors need not hold shares unless this is required by the Articles.

There is currently no minimum or maximum age limit but:

- a proposed director must be able to sign the consent to act;
- you should take legal advice if the child is very young.

The Registrar in Scotland will not register a director under 16. As from 1 October 2009 no one under the age of 16 can be a director and anyone under 16 acting as a director will be disqualified.

Some non-British citizens are excluded – so check for clearance with the Border and Immigration Agency, Lunar House, 40 Wellesley Road, Croydon CR9 2BY (tel: 0845 101 6677) or check the website, www.bia.homeoffice.gov.uk.

There is no longer a requirement that a director holds shares in the company.

Appointment of directors

The first directors are appointed by the subscribers to the Memorandum who sign the Statement of Proposed Officers filed on incorporation. Additional and subsequent appointments are made by ordinary (majority) resolution.

Directors or shareholders can recommend the appointment or reappointment of directors in a general meeting. Notice of a shareholder's proposal must, however, be served on the company between 14 and 35 days before the meeting, accompanied by a consent to act, and the company must give shareholders notice of the proposal between 7 and 28 days before the meeting.

An alternate director can be appointed by directors to attend meetings and act in their place; they are not the director's agent and are responsible for their own decisions. The directors must approve the appointment by ordinary resolution and the company must be given notice of their appointment and removal.

Details of the appointment of directors must be filed on Form 288a, signed by the officer confirming his or her consent to act, but the appointment is effective even if the notice is not filed. The resignation or retirement of directors or the secretary or changes in their particulars, however, must be filed with the Registrar on Forms 288a, 288b and 288c respectively (see pages 62–64).

Resignation and removal

If the service contract does not include notice provisions, directors can resign at any time by giving notice. Removal is by a majority vote of the shareholders and the shareholders and the director must have 28 days' notice of the proposal. The director must be notified of the resolution and can make written representations in protest. If there is sufficient time this must be sent with the notice of the proposal sent to shareholders, otherwise the director can require his representations to be read out at the meeting.

Shareholders' approval is also required for voluntary payments to directors for loss of office. A memorandum with details of the proposed payment must be available for inspection at the registered office for 15 days before the meeting or, if to be approved by written resolution, sent to shareholders with the resolution.

Approval is not required for a total payment of £200 or a pension in respect of past services.

The board of directors

Sole directors make their own decisions. If there are two or more directors they may have to work through the board which usually conducts and controls company business. The draft model Articles require a quorum of two directors – or the sole director – at meetings, but formal meetings are often dispensed with and the board can delegate its powers to one or more board members and appoint a managing director (see pages 75 and 78).

Part-time directors. Non-executive directors with financial, legal or technical expertise can be appointed.

Alternate directors who speak and act on behalf of board members in their temporary absence can be appointed if you have an appropriate provision in the Articles.

Nominee directors are appointed to represent substantial shareholders. They must not act solely in their principal's interests but, like any other director, in the interests of the company as a whole.

Shadow directors are persons in accordance with whose instructions the directors are accustomed to act and they have the same duties and obligations as any other directors. Your professional advisers, however, are not regarded as shadow directors.

Directors as employees

Directors are company employees. They have no right under the Articles to notice or compensation for loss of office but they have the same rights as other employees under the employment legislation provided they receive a salary. The draft model Articles entitle them to payment of directors' fees and payment for other services for the company as agreed by the directors or decided by ordinary shareholders' resolution, plus payment of reasonable expenses incurred in the exercise of their duties and discharge of their responsibilities as directors. They should, therefore, be employed under a service contract setting out their terms and conditions of employment, including pension arrangements, the level of contributions to be paid for life assurance and details of benefits in kind. Qualifying indemnity provisions should also be included. Aggregate directors' remuneration does not have to be included in your small company's annual accounts.

Directors and shadow directors' service contracts exceeding two years must be approved by the shareholders and can be terminated at any time on reasonable notice. The contract, or if not in writing, a memorandum setting out its terms, must be available for inspection at the registered office for at least 15 days before the shareholders' meeting or, if to be approved by written resolution, sent to shareholders with the resolution. The contract or memorandum must be available for inspection during the currency of the contract and for at least one year from the date of its termination or expiry. The Registrar must be notified of the place where the contract can be inspected.

The company and officers failing to comply with these provisions are liable to fines of up to £1,000 plus a daily default fine of up to £100.

Directors' duties

Directors are constitutional monarchs bound by the terms of the company's charter set out in the Articles. They can exercise all the powers permitted by them which are not reserved for the shareholders in general meeting. If a director is the majority shareholder and sole director, rule may be despotic.

The acts of directors are valid and cannot be set aside, even if it is later revealed that they:

- were disqualified from holding office;
- had ceased to hold office;
- were not entitled to vote on a specific resolution;
- were not appointed properly or there was a defect in their appointment.

Directors' general duties specified in the 2006 Companies Act require them to:

- act within their powers for a proper purpose and in accordance with the Articles in the management of the company's business;
- promote the company's success, by acting in good faith and in a way most likely to achieve this;
- exercise independent judgement in the interests of the company as a whole;
- exercise reasonable care, skill and diligence with the general knowledge, skill and experience reasonably expected of a director and of a person in the director's position;
- avoid conflicts of interest in dealing with third parties – their interests must not conflict with those of the company and they must not use company assets or knowledge acquired through the company for personal benefit;
- refuse benefits from third parties;
- declare their interest in proposed transactions or arrangements to the other directors. The director cannot then take part in discussing the transaction; if the director does so, the transaction can be set aside by the company. However, the director can vote in shareholders' meetings. Details may have to be included in the audited accounts. The prohibition on voting in the draft model Articles can, however, be removed by ordinary shareholders' resolution.

The directors must also comply with the general law and:

- act honestly and in good faith in the best interests of the company as a whole. This imposes a trustee's responsibility to take proper care of company assets and to ensure payments are properly made and supported by adequate documentation. They must not profit at the company's expense and must disclose their interest in company transactions to the board or general meeting; disclosure should be formally minuted;
- exercise such a degree of skill and care in carrying out their duties as might reasonably be expected from someone of their ability and experience;
- carry out the statutory obligations imposed by the Companies Act and other legislation.

Companies House
— for the record —

288a

APPOINTMENT of director or secretary

(NOT for resignation (use Form 288b) or change of particulars (use Form 288c))

Please complete in typescript, or in bold black capitals.

CHWP000

Company Number

Company Name in full

Date of appointment — Day Month Year

†Date of Birth — Day Month Year

Appointment form

Notes on completion appear on reverse.

Appointment as director

as secretary

Please mark the appropriate box. If appointment is as a director and secretary mark both boxes.

NAME *Style / Title

*Honours etc

Forename(s)

Surname

Previous Forename(s)

Previous Surname(s)

†† Tick this box if the address shown is a service address for the beneficiary of a Confidentiality Order granted under the provisions of section 723B of the Companies Act 1985

†† Usual residential address

Post town

Postcode

County / Region

Country

†Nationality

†Business occupation

†Other directorships (additional space overleaf)

I consent to act as ** director / secretary of the above named company

Consent signature

Date

* Voluntary details.
† Directors only.
**Delete as appropriate

A director, secretary etc must sign the form below.

Signed

Date

(**a director / secretary / administrator / administrative receiver / receiver manager / receiver)

You do not have to give any contact information in the box opposite but if you do, it will help Companies House to contact you if there is a query on the form. The contact information that you give will be visible to searchers of the public record..

Tel

DX number DX exchange

Companies House receipt date barcode

This form has been provided free of charge by Companies House

Form 10/03

When you have completed and signed the form please send it to the Registrar of Companies at:

Companies House, Crown Way, Cardiff, CF14 3UZ DX 33050 Cardiff
for companies registered in England and Wales or
Companies House, 37 Castle Terrace, Edinburgh, EH1 2EB
for companies registered in Scotland DX 235 Edinburgh
or LP - 4 Edinburgh 2

Figure 4.1 Appointment of a director or secretary

Companies House
— for the record —

288b

Terminating appointment as director or secretary

(NOT for appointment (use Form 288a) or change of particulars (use Form 288c))

Please complete in typescript, or in bold black capitals.

CHWP000

Company Number

Company Name in full

Day Month Year

Date of termination of appointment

as director as secretary

Please mark the appropriate box. If terminating appointment as a director and secretary mark both boxes.

NAME *Style / Title *Honours etc

Please insert details as previously notified to Companies House.

Forename(s)

Surname

Day Month Year

†Date of Birth

A serving director, secretary etc must sign the form below.

Signed **Date**

* Voluntary details.
† Directors only.
** Delete as appropriate

(** serving director / secretary / administrator / administrative receiver / receiver manager / receiver)

You do not have to give any contact information in the box opposite but if you do, it will help Companies House to contact you if there is a query on the form. The contact information that you give will be visible to searchers of the public record.

Tel

DX number DX exchange

Companies House receipt date barcode

This form has been provided free of charge by Companies House.

When you have completed and signed the form please send it to the Registrar of Companies at:

Companies House, Crown Way, Cardiff, CF14 3UZ DX 33050 Cardiff
for companies registered in England and Wales or
Companies House, 37 Castle Terrace, Edinburgh, EH1 2EB
for companies registered in Scotland DX 235 Edinburgh
or LP - 4 Edinburgh

Form revised 10/03

Figure 4.2 Resignation of a director or secretary

Companies House
— for the record —

288c

CHANGE OF PARTICULARS for director or secretary ***(NOT for appointment (use Form 288a) or resignation (use Form 288b))***

Please complete in typescript, or in bold black capitals.

CHWP000

Company Number

Company Name in full

Changes of particulars form *Complete in all cases*

Date of change of particulars — Day Month Year

Name *Style / Title — *Honours etc

Forename(s)

Surname

† Date of Birth — Day Month Year

Change of name *(enter new name)* Forename(s)

Surname

Change of usual residential address ††

(enter new address)

†† Tick this box if the address shown is a service address for the beneficiary of a Confidentiality Order granted under the provisions of section 723B of the Companies Act 1985

Post town

County / Region — Postcode

Country

Other change *(please specify)*

A serving director, secretary etc must sign the form below.

Signed — **Date**

(** director / secretary / administrator / administrative receiver / receiver manager / receiver)

* Voluntary details.
† Directors only.
**Delete as appropriate.

You do not have to give any contact information in the box opposite but if you do, it will help Companies House to contact you if there is a query on the form. The contact information that you give will be visible to searchers of the public record..

Tel

DX number — DX exchange

Companies House receipt date barcode

This form has been provided free of charge by Companies House

Form 10/03

When you have completed and signed the form please send it to the Registrar of Companies at:

Companies House, Crown Way, Cardiff, CF14 3UZ — DX 33050 Cardiff
for companies registered in England and Wales — or
Companies House, 37 Castle Terrace, Edinburgh, EH1 2EB
for companies registered in Scotland — DX 235 Edinburgh or LP - 4 Edinburgh 2

Figure 4.3 Change of particulars for a director or secretary

Directors as agents

Because the company is a separate legal entity, directors can only act as the company's agents, acting on their principal's (the company's) instructions, express or implied. For instance, a director's signature on a company contract binds the company, but if they sign contracts in their own name, without any reference to the company, they can be personally liable under the contract.

Loans to directors and 'connected persons'

The following loans, credit transactions, and quasi-loans – a payment made on behalf of a director to a third party where the borrower is liable to reimburse the creditor – require no approval:

- loans etc up to £50,000 for a director's expenditure on company business;
- loans to fund a director's defence in a regulatory authority's investigation;
- loans and quasi-loans up to £10,000;
- credit transactions up to of £15,000;
- credit transactions, loans and quasi-loans made by a moneylending company, in the ordinary course of business on the same terms and no greater than the company or moneylending company would have offered to an independent third party of the same financial standing;
- home loans by a moneylending company in the ordinary course of its business for the borrower's principal private residence on the company's usual terms for loans to employees.

Loans to directors, and guarantees and security given by a director in connection with loans made to a third party, must be approved by shareholders within a reasonable period after the transaction is entered into. The shareholders must receive a memorandum setting out:

- the nature of the transaction;
- the amount of the loan and its purpose;
- the extent of the company's liability.

This must be available for inspection 15 days before the meeting at the registered office, or if to be approved by written resolution, sent to shareholders with the resolution.

Arrangements for anyone to make a loan or give collateral for a director in return for a benefit from the company also requires shareholders' approval.

If the company fails to comply with the procedures, the transaction can be set aside and the director may have to account to the company for any profit.

Connected persons

Persons 'connected with' a director comprise the director's business or professional partner, spouse, civil partner or person with whom the director or shadow director lives as partner in an enduring family relationship, that partner's child or step-child under the age of 18 who lives with the director or shadow director, and the director or shadow director's child, step-child or parents.

Also included is any company with which the director is associated and of which the director controls at least one-fifth of the votes at general meetings, any trustee of any trust under which the director, the above family group or the associated companies are beneficiaries, and any partner of a 'connected person'.

A trust under which ALL the employees can obtain shares is not a 'connected person'.

Loans to employees

There is no top limit on an advance made to set up a trust to buy shares in the company for employees, including full-time salaried directors, or on the amount employees may borrow to buy company shares. The company can, however, assist anyone in the purchase of its shares, provided that the company's assets are not thereby reduced or, to the extent of the reduction, the finance comes out of distributable profits.

The assistance can be by gift, loan guarantee, security, indemnity or any other financial help which materially reduces the net assets.

The smaller business has some tax concessions here but the statutory provisions are complicated and you should seek expert advice before calling on your company's generosity.

The Consumer Credit Act 1974

Transactions of under £25,000, including the cost of the credit, must comply with the terms of the Consumer Credit Act 1974.

Company non-cash assets

A non-cash asset is property or an interest in property, other than cash. It is substantial if at the time of the arrangement it is worth more than £100,000 or 10 per cent of the company's net assets as shown in the accounts, or, if accounts have not been produced, 10 per cent of the called up share capital.

Shareholders' approval is required if directors and shadow directors or their 'connections' (see page 66) acquire a substantial non-cash asset from the company or the company acquires a substantial non-cash asset from them.

Failing proper disclosure and the shareholders' approval, the transaction can be set aside and the director or shadow director may have to account to the company for any profit.

Shareholder's approval, however, is not required if the company is in administration or being wound up, unless it is a shareholders' voluntary winding up (see Chapter 7).

Fines and penalties

Credit facilities extended in contravention of the legislation can be cancelled by the company. The company is entitled to reimbursement unless this is impossible, or the company has been indemnified for loss and damage, or an outsider without knowledge of the contravention might suffer loss. If restitution is not possible, the contravenor and any director authorising the transaction are liable to reimburse or indemnify the company. In addition, they have to recompense it for any consequential gain or loss unless they can prove they did not know the transaction was unlawful. If the transaction is with a director's connection, the connected director is not liable if he or she took all reasonable steps to ensure that the company complied with the Companies Acts.

There is no way to save an unlawful transfer of assets by providing an indemnity through a third party.

Share dealings

There is no restriction on directors' share and debenture dealings, as long as the company is kept informed and details entered on the company's Register of Directors' Interests.

Skill and care

Directors must exercise the degree of skill and care that may reasonably be expected from someone in their position with their ability and experience. Professionally qualified directors must therefore act with the care and diligence expected from a member of their profession and, unless they are part-time directors, should devote themselves full time to the job.

Non-executive directors are usually not involved in day-to-day management and the only requirement is that they regularly attend board meetings. They must exercise an independent standard of judgement and if they are properly to fulfil the purpose of their appointment they should be encouraged to participate fully in board decisions.

Delegation

The directors can delegate their duties but they must be satisfied that they are delegating to a suitable person who is competent, reliable and honest. They cannot simply abandon responsibility but must keep themselves informed as to progress.

Statutory duties

The directors' *administrative duties* are contained mainly in the Companies Acts and the Insolvency Act 1986.

Both the company and its officers can be fined for failure to comply with the statutory requirements, and persistent default can lead to disqualification from acting as a director or from being involved in company management for up to 15 years, or imprisonment. Fines, payable on demand, apply to the late filing of accounts. They range from £100 for accounts delivered up to three months late to £500 for a delay of over 6 months filed before 1 February 2009. After 1 February 2009 fines range from £150 for accounts delivered up to a month late to £1,500 for a delay of over 6 months. These are in addition to fines imposed on the directors in the criminal courts. The company can be struck off if both the accounts and the annual return are not filed on time; the directors may face disqualification, a criminal conviction and a fine if they fail to file the statutory documents. Directors of small companies therefore often pass these duties to their accountants or solicitors (who are experienced in company administration) so that they can concentrate on management. This is an appropriate delegation of duty but the directors are still required to supervise and they are ultimately responsible for ensuring that the company complies with legal requirements.

The company secretary, if any, is responsible for maintaining the statutory documents and registers, but the directors must ensure that the company keeps proper records and files the necessary documentation with the Registrar.

Directors' liability

Limited liability means that the company is responsible for business debts and obligations. Liability can, however, be passed to directors and management.

The draft model Articles state that directors are responsible for the management of the company's business, for which purpose they may exercise all the powers of the company. They therefore have unlimited powers to bind/act on behalf of the company and to authorise others to do so, subject to the restrictions imposed by the Articles, provided everyone is acting in good faith. Outsiders are not required to enquire whether their powers are restricted by the Articles.

Private companies can also give directors prospective authorisation to act in breach of their duty to avoid conflicts of interest unless this is forbidden under the Articles.

Breach of statutory or other duty and fraud are defined in the 2006 Fraud Act as:

- making a false representation;
- failing to disclose information where there is a legal or other duty to disclose;
- abusing a position as director or other company executive.

The Act also creates two new offences:

- obtaining services dishonestly;
- possessing, making and supplying articles for use in fraud.

However, the directors are only liable for negligence if they are clearly at fault and the company cannot exempt them from, or indemnify them against, any liability in connection with negligence, default, breach of duty or breach of trust.

BUT directors and company officers can be indemnified out of the company's assets against liability incurred in defending civil or criminal proceedings if they obtain judgment.

Directors may also be liable personally if they act outside the powers given by the Articles or if they contract without reference to the company by, for instance, placing orders without stating that they are acting on behalf of the company. They are also liable on cheques and other negotiable instruments which do not carry the company's full registered name.

Directors are liable for 'misfeasance' (wrongdoing): for instance, making secret profits at the company's expense. 'Nonfeasance' (doing nothing), however, may bring no liability unless it comes within the matters to be considered on an application for disqualification. A director can apply to the court for relief in any proceedings for negligence, default, breach of duty or trust, and the court will relieve him or her of liability if satisfied that he or she acted reasonably and honestly and, in the circumstances, ought fairly to be excused.

Employers' duties

The legal obligations imposed on employers relating to employees and third parties affected by the company's business activities apply to all employers. Because of the protection of limited liability, claims are made against the company. Although the directors are responsible for ensuring compliance with the law, liability is only passed to them if there is fraud or, in some circumstances, negligence.

The directors, the company and the shareholders

Minority shareholders have no say in the running of the business, and if management is inefficient they may be able to do nothing. It is only the company itself – that is, the majority shareholders, or, in some circumstances 75 per cent of the shareholders – who can take action. Provided directors act in good faith and in the interests of the company as a whole, the majority shareholders can do anything permitted by the Articles and can ratify almost any transaction, even retrospectively.

A single current and former shareholder can, however, sue the company in his or her own name to protect individual rights, for example to compel the board to accept their vote at general meetings, or if they consider themselves to be 'unfairly prejudiced' by the way in which the company's affairs have been, are being, or will be conducted.

They can also bring a 'derivative' claim. This is brought on behalf of the company under the 2006 Act and is based on an actual or proposed act or omission involving negligence, default, breach of duty or breach of trust by a director or directors. The company must be notified when proceedings take place and the shareholder must apply to the court for permission to continue the claim. Permission to continue is based on prima facie evidence – evidence adequate to prove the conduct complained of – and the court must consider whether:

- the claimant or claimants are acting in good faith;
- the company has decided not to pursue the claim;
- the claimant(s) could instead continue the proceedings in their own right rather than on behalf of the company.

The court must have 'particular regard to any evidence as to the views' of shareholders with no personal interests, direct or indirect, in the claim, and permission will be refused if the court is satisfied that someone acting in accordance with the duty to promote the company's success would not make the claim, or the company authorised or ratified the action complained of. If the application is dismissed, the court may order the claimant to pay costs. The claimant has seven days to ask for an oral hearing to reconsider the decision and if it succeeds the company may be ordered to pay both sides' costs.

In addition, the draft model Articles give shareholders a 'reserve power' to compel the directors by special resolution to take, or refrain from taking, specified action, although the resolution does not invalidate anything the directors have already done. They can also ratify the negligence, default, breach of duty or breach of trust of directors, former directors and shadow directors in relation to the company by special resolution. The company then has no claim against those directors and any shareholders involved or against directors connected with them. If the company brings a claim against them, they are not liable if the court finds they acted honestly and reasonably.

Insurance is obtainable for indemnities against claims brought by shareholders.

Directors and outsiders

Third party claims on directors are usually made by unpaid creditors when the company goes into insolvent liquidation and the protection of limited liability is lost if there has been fraudulent or wrongful trading. Liability can fall on non-executive shadow and nominee directors, as well as full-time working directors.

Fraudulent trading is trading with intent to defraud creditors. It can arise when cheques are paid into the company's bank account after a company stops trading, even if paid in under the genuine and reasonable belief that creditors will be paid in a short time. Floating charges and loans are invalid if made within six months of a winding up, unless the company was solvent when the loan was made; in some circumstances the directors must repay the creditor and may also be liable to prosecution.

Wrongful trading. Penalties here extend to disqualification and imprisonment but only if it is proved that at some time before the liquidation the company was trading although the director knew, or ought to have known, that there was no reasonable prospect that it could avoid insolvent liquidation.

For 12 months after insolvent liquidation the directors and shadow directors cannot act for a company with the same name. The court's consent is required before they act for a company using its former name or trading name or one suggesting a continuing association with it.

Personal guarantees are a problem only when the company cannot pay its debts. A guarantee on the bank overdraft is probably the most usual undertaking required from directors in support of a company. This is often backed up by a charge on a director's home. The bank usually requires the director's spouse to be a joint and several guarantor to give the bank priority to the spouse's claim to the equity in the property. A director is advised to resist a request for a charge on personal assets, particularly on his or her home, as a charge given for business purposes removes the protection under the general law given to residential owners. Independent legal advice should be sought before any guarantees are given.

Business leases

Landlords often require directors to join in a lease of company premises as surety. If the company cannot pay rent, the landlord can then turn to the directors for payment and they remain liable until the lease expires, even if the lease is assigned or the landlord consents to their release.

The terms of the lease may require companies qualifying for the audit exemption to produce audited accounts.

Commercial contracts

Finance companies often require directors to guarantee payments made by the company on instalment contracts. The contracts provide that in the event of premature termination, the full balance is immediately due and payable, and the directors are liable to pay the full amount if the company cannot do so.

Insurance

The company can indemnify its officers and auditors against liability for negligence, default, breach of duty and breach of trust. The cover is for both civil and criminal proceedings, provided judgment is given in their favour, they are acquitted or relief is granted by the court. You may want to arrange additional insurance to cover the unindemnifiable risk, with the party at risk paying an appropriate proportion of the premium.

The Articles must, however, include an appropriate provision giving the company the power to purchase the insurance, and details of the insurance must be included in the directors' report.

Disqualification

Directors may be disqualified:

- on conviction for an offence connected with the promotion, formation, management or liquidation of the company;
- on conviction for an offence connected with the receivership of the company's property or with being an administrative receiver of the company;
- if guilty of a fraud in relation to the company;
- for non-compliance with the Companies Acts, but there must have been 'persistent default', that is, at least three offences within five years.

Disqualification can be for up to 15 years and the court has discretion as to whether or not to make the order. It must, however, disqualify directors whose conduct in relation to the company, alone or together with their conduct as directors of another company, makes them, in the court's opinion, unfit to be concerned in the management of a company.

The Register of Disqualification Orders, maintained by the Secretary of State, is open to public inspection. Anyone acting while disqualified is jointly and severally liable with the company employing him or her for debts incurred during the period of disqualification, and liability extends to anyone acting on their instructions.

The Companies House Disqualified Directors List gives details of disqualification orders for directors in England, Wales and Scotland. It is updated regularly.

5

Running the company

The price of limited liability is a certain amount of publicity – documentation and reports must be sent to the Companies Registry, where some are available for public inspection on payment of a fee. In addition, you must make regular reports to shareholders and accounts must conform with the requirements of the Companies Acts.

Notices, accounts and reports can be filed with Companies House electronically or via post, fax or e-mail. Companies House recommends WebFiling as a safe, reliable and cheaper method of filing company information. Data can be filed online between 7.00am and midnight every day except Sunday and you can sign up to PROOF to protect yourself from corporate identity theft for no extra charge.

You must first register for a Security Code – which is e-mailed to you – and then register for an Authentication Code, which is posted to the company's registered office. A list of the documents you can file online is listed on the Companies House website and their User Guide gives details and directions.

Accounts, summary financial statements and reports can also be sent electronically to shareholders, debenture-holders and auditors. Provided that you notify the recipients, they can also be published on your website. Announcement that notices are on a website must contain specified details about meetings and your shareholders can send proxy forms and other notices to you via e-mail.

Directors

You may want to appoint one of the directors as managing director or executive director, although they have no specific powers under the Companies Acts.

Recruitment – getting it right

Where do I advertise? What words should I use? What skills do the applicants need to have? Do I need to tell them why they didn't get the job?

These are just some of the questions employers ask us when they are planning to recruit new staff. Although recruitment is a sign that your business is growing it can cause a lot of anxiety.

Some employers are worried about discriminating against an applicant by using the wrong words in the advert. Other employers are so concerned about filling a post quickly they fail to get someone with the right skills and have to repeat the process.

Thinking it through from the start can save you a great deal of time and money further down the line. Acas can help you get it right.

Your recruitment checklist.

You need to:

- write an accurate job description
- draw up a person specification which identifies the necessary and desirable qualifications, skills and experience needed to fill the post
- advertise the job to the widest possible audience
- ensure that you have appropriate recruitment procedures and that they do not discriminate on the grounds of age, race, disability, gender, sexual orientation, religion or belief
- check your staff are eligible to work in the UK – if they're not, you could be fined
- make sure that new employees have a properly planned induction
- give every employee a written statement of employment within two months of starting.

Acas offers information and advice on recruitment, selection and induction. Go to **www.acas.org.uk** for advice on this topic, to book training or order our guide *Recruitment and induction.*

advertisement feature

Their authority is based entirely on the terms and conditions of their service contract or those imposed by the board.

The draft model Articles enable the directors to delegate their powers to a managing director or chief executive officer who frequently chairs board and general meetings. The chair can be appointed at each meeting and is given an extra, casting, vote if there is deadlock.

The company secretary

Your private company no longer needs a company secretary. If you appoint one, he or she must be named in the documents lodged prior to registration and the appointment should be minuted at the first directors' meeting. The company secretary can also be a director, provided he or she is not the sole director.

The draft model Articles provide that the company secretary be appointed and removed by the directors for such a term at such remuneration and on such conditions as they may think fit.

The company secretary is the company's chief administrative officer responsible for maintaining and updating the statutory registers and documents and with ostensible authority in day-to-day administrative matters, including convening board and company meetings, taking minutes of meetings, filing returns, accounts and forms with the Registrar, and dealing with share transfers and proxies.

The directors are, however, ultimately responsible for ensuring that the statutory registers and documents are up to date and meetings minuted, whether or not the company has a company secretary.

The statutory records

The company must keep certain registers and documents which must be filed with the Registrar. They must also be made available for inspection electronically and at the registered office or address designated by the directors.

Anyone can inspect the following documents; there is no charge to shareholders but outsiders pay a minimum fee of £3.50 for inspection and copies.

The *Register of Shareholders*, which lists the names and addresses of the subscribers to the Memorandum of Association and the shareholders.

The Register of Directors, with the directors' forenames, surnames and former names (ie any names used for business purposes before the age of 16 or during the 20 years prior to registration), nationality, business occupation and details of any other directorships held within the previous five years and their address, which can be the registered office address.

The *Register of Directors' Residential Addresses* must also be filed with the Registrar. But this constitutes 'protected information' if supplied as such on Forms 10 and 288a and may not be used or disclosed except:

- to communicate with the director;
- to report changes in the register to the Registrar;
- to comply with a court order;
- with the director's consent;
- at the request of certain public authorities;
- at the request of a credit reference agency.

The address remains protected after the director ceases to hold office. If information on the Register of Directors of the Register of Directors' Residential Addresses is inaccurate the company and its officers, including shadow directors, may be fined up to £5.000 plus a daily default fine of up to £500.

The Register of Secretaries if you appoint a company secretary – with present and former forenames, and the address for service of company documents. This can again be the registered office address.

The Register of Charges with details of mortgages and fixed and floating charges secured on the company's assets, consisting of a short description of the property charged, the amount of the charge and the names of the lenders, except in the case of securities to bearer. Copies must also be available for inspection and available for copying by shareholders, creditors and outsiders.

You are not required to keep a *Register of Debentures,* but if you do so, it must be available for inspection.

Documents that may be inspected ONLY by shareholders and creditors:

The directors' statement and auditors' report supplied in connection with a payment out of the company's capital for the redemption or purchase of the company's shares must be available for inspection for five weeks after the resolution to make the payment.

Documents and records that may ONLY be inspected by shareholders without charge, copies of which must be provided on payment of a fee:

Directors' and shadow directors' service contracts exceeding two years. The full written contract, if any, must be available for at least a year from the date of termination of the contract. Otherwise you must supply a written memorandum setting out its terms.

Records of resolutions and meetings and relevant documents must be available for 10 years.

The company's written contract to purchase its own shares, or memorandum of its terms, must be available for 10 years after the date of completion or termination of the contract.

Shareholders can also request copies of the company's Memorandum of Association and Articles.

The company's accounting records can ONLY be inspected by company officers. They must be kept at the registered office or other place designated by the directors and must be open for inspection at all times.

Annual return

Each year an annual return must be filed with the Registrar on Form 363a (see pages 82–87), Companies House notifies the registered office when the annual return is due to be filed. It can be filed electronically; if you prefer to file a paper annual return you must order it by telephone on 0870 33 33 636.

The return is made up to the 'return date', which is the anniversary of the date of incorporation.

The return must include a statement of capital and state:

- the company's name, registered number and registered office address;
- that it is private;
- its principal business activity;
- the name and address of the company secretary, if any;
- the name, address, date of birth, nationality and business occupation of the directors;
- the address where the Registers of Shareholders and Register of Debentures if any are kept, if not at the registered office;
- the shareholders' names, addresses and the number of shares of each class they hold. Thereafter these need only be given in every third annual return, with intermediate returns setting out changes since the previous return;
- the names and addresses of shareholders who have ceased to be members and the number of shares of each class which they have transferred since the date of incorporation (or, in subsequent returns, since the date to which the previous return was made up);
- the date to which the annual return is made up (the made-up date).

Appointment of new directors, however, must be filed on Form 288a and the resignation or retirement of directors or the secretary and changes in their particulars on Forms 288b and 288c respectively (see pages 63–64) A change in the registered office address must be filed on Form 287.

The classification of the company's principal business activities is based on the UK Standard Industrial Classification Codes (SIC 03), a numerical classification of companies' principal business activities, including sub-class revisions effective from 1 January 2003. The latest version of the code, SIC 2007, will be adopted when the new IT system is up and running at Companies House.

A copy of the annual return signed by a director or the secretary, if any, must be sent to the Registrar, with the registration fee of £30, or £15 if filed electronically, within 28 days of the return date.

Companies House will send you its 'shuttle' Annual Return Form 363a for following years.

If an annual return is not filed, the company, the directors and company secretary, if any, are liable to criminal prosecution and fines of up to £1,000.

The accounts

Accounting reference date

Your newly incorporated company's accounting reference date (ARD) – the date to which it will make up accounts each year – is the last day of the month in which the anniversary of incorporation falls plus or minus seven days. For instance, a company incorporated on 16 April 2003 would have an ARD of 30 April and its accounts would cover the period from 30 April 2003 to 30 April 2004, plus or minus seven days. Accounts filed with a made-up date other than the ARD will be rejected by the Registrar and the company and directors will be liable to fines.

The first accounting reference period starts on incorporation and the first accounts can cover a period of between 6 and 18 months. If they cover 12 months or fewer they must be delivered to the Registrar within 9 months of the accounting reference date (ARD) – the date on which the accounting reference period ends. If the accounts cover more than 12 months, they must be filed 3 months after the end of the ARD, or the anniversary of the date of incorporation, whichever is later.

Deadlines are calculated to the exact day. If the first ARD is 30 September 2008, you have until midnight on 30 December 2009, NOT 31 December, to deliver the first account covering a period of over 12 months; if the filing date is a Sunday or bank holiday they must arrive BEFORE the specified date.

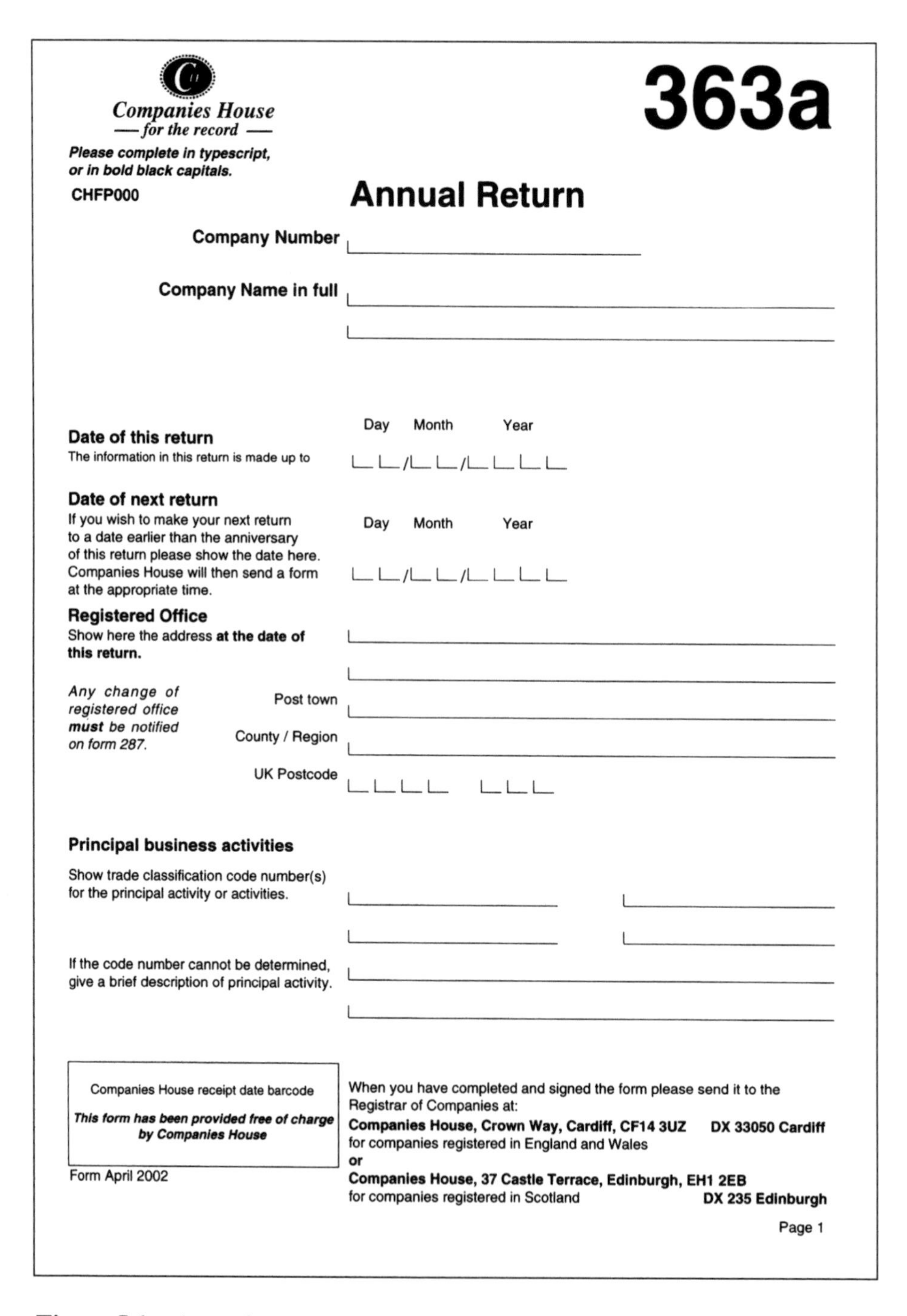

Companies House
— for the record —

Please complete in typescript, or in bold black capitals.

CHFP000

363a

Annual Return

Company Number

Company Name in full

Date of this return
The information in this return is made up to

Day Month Year

Date of next return
If you wish to make your next return to a date earlier than the anniversary of this return please show the date here. Companies House will then send a form at the appropriate time.

Day Month Year

Registered Office
Show here the address **at the date of this return.**

*Any change of registered office **must** be notified on form 287.*

Post town

County / Region

UK Postcode

Principal business activities

Show trade classification code number(s) for the principal activity or activities.

If the code number cannot be determined, give a brief description of principal activity.

Companies House receipt date barcode

This form has been provided free of charge by Companies House

Form April 2002

When you have completed and signed the form please send it to the Registrar of Companies at:

Companies House, Crown Way, Cardiff, CF14 3UZ DX 33050 Cardiff
for companies registered in England and Wales
or
Companies House, 37 Castle Terrace, Edinburgh, EH1 2EB
for companies registered in Scotland **DX 235 Edinburgh**

Page 1

Figure 5.1 Annual return

Register of members

If the register of members is not kept at the registered office, state here where it is kept.

Post town

County / Region UK Postcode

Register of Debenture holders

If there is a register of debenture holders, or a duplicate of any such register or part of it, which is not kept at the registered office, state here where it is kept.

Post town

County / Region UK Postcode

Company type

Public limited company

Private company limited by shares

Private company limited by guarantee without share capital

Private company limited by shares exempt under section 30

Private company limited by guarantee exempt under section 30

Private unlimited company with share capital

Private unlimited company without share capital

Please tick the appropriate box

Company Secretary

* Voluntary details.

(Please photocopy this area to provide details of joint secretaries).

Details of a new company secretary must be notified on form 288a.

Name * Style / Title

Forename(s)

Surname

Address ††

Post town

County / Region UK Postcode

Country

†† Tick this box if the address shown is a service address for the beneficiary of a Confidentiality Order granted under section 723B of the Companies Act 1985 otherwise, give your usual residential address. In the case of a corporation or Scottish firm, give the registered or principal office address.

If a partnership give the names and addresses of the partners or the name of the partnership and office address.

Page 2

Figure 5.1 *continued*

Directors

Please list directors in alphabetical order.

Details of new directors must be notified on form 288a

Name * Style / Title

Directors In the case of a director that is a corporation or a Scottish firm, the name is the corporate or firm name.

Day Month Year

Date of birth __ __ / __ __ / __ __ __ __

Forename(s)

Surname

†† Tick this box if the address shown is a service address for the beneficiary of a Confidentiality Order granted under section 723B of the Companies Act 1985 otherwise, give your usual residential address. In the case of a corporation or Scottish firm, give the registered or principal office address.

Address ††

Post town

County / Region

UK Postcode

Country

Nationality

Business occupation

* Voluntary details.

Name * Style / Title

Directors In the case of a director that is a corporation or a Scottish firm, the name is the corporate or firm name.

Day Month Year

Date of birth __ __ / __ __ / __ __ __ __

Forename(s)

Surname

†† Tick this box if the address shown is a service address for the beneficiary of a Confidentiality Order granted under section 723B of the Companies Act 1985 otherwise, give your usual residential address. In the case of a corporation or Scottish firm, give the registered or principal office address.

Address ††

Post town

County / Region

UK Postcode

Country

Nationality

Business occupation

Page 3

Figure 5.1 *continued*

Issued share capital
Enter details of all the shares in issue at the date of this return.

	Class *(e.g. Ordinary/Preference)*	Number of shares issued	Aggregate Nominal Value *(i.e Number of shares issued multiplied by nominal value per share, or total amount of stock)*
	Totals		

List of past and present shareholders
(Use attached schedule where appropriate)
A full list is required if one was not included with either of the last two returns.

There were no changes in the period ☐

	on paper	in another format
A list of changes is enclosed	☐	☐
A full list of shareholders is enclosed	☐	☐

Certificate

I certify that the information given in this return is true to the best of my knowledge and belief.

Signed ____________ **Date** ____________

† Please delete as appropriate.

† a director /secretary

When you have signed the return send it with the fee to the Registrar of Companies. Cheques should be made payable to **Companies House.**

This return includes ☐ continuation sheets.
(enter number)

You do not have to give any contact information in the box opposite but if you do, it will help Companies House to contact you if there is a query on the form. The contact information that you give will be visible to searchers of the public record.

Tel

DX number DX exchange

Page 4

Figure 5.1 *continued*

Directors

Please list directors in alphabetical order.

Details of new directors must be notified on form 288a

Name * Style / Title

Directors In the case of a director that is a corporation or a Scottish firm, the name is the corporate or firm name.

Day Month Year

Date of birth __ __ / __ __ / __ __ __ __

Forename(s)

Surname

Address ††

†† Tick this box if the address shown is a service address for the beneficiary of a Confidentiality Order granted under section 723B of the Companies Act 1985 otherwise, give your usual residential address. In the case of a corporation or Scottish firm, give the registered or principal office address.

Post town

County / Region

UK Postcode __ __ __ __ __ __ __

Country

Nationality

Business occupation

* Voluntary details.

Name * Style / Title

Directors In the case of a director that is a corporation or a Scottish firm, the name is the corporate or firm name.

Day Month Year

Date of birth __ __ / __ __ / __ __ __ __

Forename(s)

Surname

Address ††

†† Tick this box if the address shown is a service address for the beneficiary of a Confidentiality Order granted under section 723B of the Companies Act 1985 otherwise, give your usual residential address. In the case of a corporation or Scottish firm, give the registered or principal office address.

Post town

County / Region

UK Postcode __ __ __ __ __ __ __

Country

Nationality

Business occupation

Page 5

Figure 5.1 *continued*

Directors

Details of new directors must be notified on form 288a

Please list directors in alphabetical order.

Name * Style / Title

Directors In the case of a director that is a corporation or a Scottish firm, the name is the corporate or firm name.

Day Month Year

Date of birth

Forename(s)

Surname

†† Tick this box if the address shown is a service address for the beneficiary of a Confidentiality Order granted under section 723B of the Companies Act 1985 otherwise, give your usual residential address. In the case of a corporation or Scottish firm, give the registered or principal office address.

Address ††

Post town

County / Region

UK Postcode

Country

Nationality

Business occupation

* Voluntary details.

Name * Style / Title

Directors In the case of a director that is a corporation or a Scottish firm, the name is the corporate or firm name.

Day Month Year

Date of birth

Forename(s)

Surname

†† Tick this box if the address shown is a service address for the beneficiary of a Confidentiality Order granted under section 723B of the Companies Act 1985 otherwise, give your usual residential address. In the case of a corporation or Scottish firm, give the registered or principal office address.

Address ††

Post town

County / Region

UK Postcode

Country

Nationality

Business occupation

Page 6

Figure 5.1 *continued*

Accounting records

The 2006 Companies Act requires companies to keep adequate accounting records to:

- show and explain the company's transactions;
- disclose with reasonable accuracy the company's current financial position;
- enable the directors to ensure that the accounts comply with the Act or, if applicable, Article 4 of the IAS Regulation (see page 89).

Records must be maintained on a day-to-day basis, including:

- details of daily cash receipts and payments, including the transactions to which they relate;
- daily entries of cash receipts and expenditure, including the transactions to which they relate;
- a list of assets and liabilities;
- if applicable, a statement of stock of goods held at the end of each (financial) year, including statements of stocktakings;
- with the exception of retailers, a sufficient description of goods and services bought and sold to enable sellers and purchasers to be identified.

The company's officers are liable to fines and/or up to two years' imprisonment if the accounts or records are inadequate unless they can prove they acted honestly.

They are also liable for up to two years' imprisonment and/or a fine if records are not available for inspection by company officers for at least three years at the registered office or other place the directors designate. If registered for VAT, records must be retained for at least six years. All these records must also be available electronically.

Copies of the company's accounts signed by a director or secretary, if any, comprise:

- the profit and loss account;
- the balance sheet approved by the board and signed by a director;
- if appropriate (see below), a special signed and dated auditors' or accountants' report;
- the director's report signed by a director or the secretary, if any;
- notes to the accounts.

Accounts must state whether they are based on the EU International Accounting Standards (IAS) or UK GAPP. Statements and filing exemptions must appear above the director's signature.

Twenty-one days before the meeting copies must be sent to all share and debenture holders and to anyone else entitled to be given notice of the meeting, such as the auditors, and copies must be sent to the Registrar. Share and debenture holders are also entitled to receive a free copy of the company's previous accounts. There is, however, no requirement to lay the accounts before the shareholders or agree them with the Inland Revenue before they are filed.

The directors are liable to fines of up to £1,000 for delay in filing the accounts with the Registrar, depending on the length of the delay (see Appendix 4). Companies House sends a reminder before the deadline, which shows the filing deadline date in bold type. If the accounts are not filed on time a default notice and a demand for payment of the fine is delivered to the company's registered office within 14 days. Appeals against the fine are made first to the Registrar, then to the Complaints Adjudicator and thereafter to the county court.

The accounts can be in English but can be in Welsh or an EU language if annexed to a certified English translation and Form 1006.

Privacy

'Small' companies with a turnover not exceeding £6.5 million, assets not exceeding £3.26 million and an average of no more than 50 employees can file unaudited accounts, or abbreviated accounts and reports, so that some details of the company's affairs remain confidential. Fulfilment of at least two of the criteria is sufficient to categorise the company.

The full accounts, the directors' report and (unless the company is exempt from audit) the auditors' report must be sent to shareholders, debenture holders and anyone entitled to receive notice of meetings.

A summary financial statement can, however, be sent to anyone who does not want to receive full details. This must state it is a summary of the information and include a statement by the auditors that it is consistent with the full accounts and reports and complies with section 427 of the 2006 Act. The auditor must also state whether their report was unqualified, in which case the full auditors' report must be annexed to the summary financial statement, together with relevant material, and the auditors must state whether or not the accounting records were adequate or the accounts did not agree with the accounting records.

The audit exemption

As from 6 April 2008 the unaudited balance sheet with explanatory notes must include a statement by the directors stating that:

- for the year ending _____ the company was entitled to the audit exemption under section 477 of the Companies Act 2006 relating to small companies;
- the shareholders have not required the company to obtain an audit of its accounts for the year in question in accordance with section 476;
- the directors acknowledge their responsibilities for complying with the requirements of the Act with respect to accounting records and the preparation of accounts.

(The audit exemption applies to company tax returns (CT600), so unaudited accounts can also be sent to HM Revenue & Customs (HMRC).

At least 10 per cent of the holders of any class of share can demand an audit by written notice to the registered office at least one month before the end of the financial year. Some companies may have to produce audited accounts to comply with the terms of their lease.

Abbreviated accounts

The abbreviated balance sheet must be filed with a special auditors' report, unless the directors were able to gain audit exemption. You are not required to file the profit and loss account.

For accounting periods starting on or after 6 April 2008, the auditors must include a statement that in their opinion the company is entitled to deliver abbreviated accounts in accordance with Section 441(1) of the Companies Act 2006 and that they have been properly prepared in accordance with the regulations made by the Secretary of State.

If the report was qualified, the full auditors' report must be annexed to relevant documents explaining the qualification. If the company has not kept proper accounting records or the auditors failed to obtain sufficient information and explanations, this must be stated in the report.

The directors' report, approved by the board and signed by a director or the secretary, need not be filed with the small company's accounts, but the directors must report to shareholders. The report must name the directors and state the company's principal activities and any change in the activities during the year.

Unless the company is exempt from auditing requirements the report must also contain:

- a statement by each director in office when the report is approved that so far as the director is aware, there is no relevant audit information of which the auditors are unaware (needed by the auditors when preparing their report);
- a statement that the director has taken all necessary steps to make him- or herself aware of relevant audit information and to establish that the company's auditors are aware of it – ie in the discharge of the director's duty to exercise due care, skill and diligence – and has made specific enquiries of the other directors and the auditors.

The report must also contain a statement in a prominent position above the signature(s) that it was prepared in accordance with the small companies regime. The auditors must also state in their report whether in their opinion the information in the directors' report is consistent with the accounts.

If the directors fail to comply with the requirements, or they knew or ought to have known that their statements were false or reckless as to whether they were false, they may be liable to fines and up to 2 years' imprisonment.

Details will be given on the Companies House and BERR websites of regulations under the 2006 Act specifying other items to be included in the directors' report which were previously required under the 1985 Companies Act.

Disclosing the accounts

The company's accounting records must be kept at the registered office or another office designated by the directors and be open to inspection by the company's officers at all times.

It is an offence to mislead the auditors and they are entitled to access to all the necessary documents and information in the preparation of the accounts.

Auditors

The auditors can be appointed by the directors before the first general meeting at which the accounts are to be presented. If no auditors are appointed, the shareholders can appoint them at any time before the beginning of the first

Companies House
— for the record —

225

Please complete in typescript, or in bold black capitals

CHWP000

Change of accounting reference date

Company Number

Company Name in Full

NOTES

You may use this form to change the accounting date relating to either the current or the immediately previous accounting period.

a. You **may not** change a period for which the accounts are already overdue.

b. You **may not** extend a period beyond 18 months unless the company is subject to an administration order.

c. You **may not** extend periods more than once in five years unless:

1. the company is subject to an administration order, or
2. you have the specific approval of the Secretary of State, (please enclose a copy), or
3. you are extending the company's accounting reference period to align with that of a parent or subsidiary undertaking established in the European Economic Area, or
4. the form is being submitted by an oversea company.

The accounting reference period ending — Day Month Year

is **shortened** ☐ **extended** ☐ so as to end on — Day Month Year

please tick appropriate box

Subsequent periods will end on the same day and month in future years.

If extending more than once in five years, please indicate in the box the number of the provision listed in note c. on which you are relying.

Signed **Date**

† Please delete as appropriate

† a director / secretary / administrator / administrative receiver / receiver and manager / receiver (Scotland) / person authorised on behalf of an oversea company

You do not have to give any contact information in the box opposite but if you do, it will help Companies House to contact you if there is a query on the form. The contact information that you give will be visible to searchers of the public record.

Tel

DX number DX exchange

Companies House receipt date barcode

This form has been provided free of charge by Companies House.

10/03

When you have completed and signed the form please send it to the Registrar of Companies at:

Companies House, Crown Way, Cardiff, CF14 3UZ **DX 33050 Cardiff**
for companies registered in England and Wales **or**
Companies House, 37 Castle Terrace, Edinburgh, EH1 2EB **DX 235 Edinburgh or LP - 4 Edinburgh 2**
for companies registered in Scotland

Figure 5.2 Change of accounting reference date

Company Number

† Directors only. †Other directorships

NOTES
Show the full forenames, NOT INITIALS. If the director or secretary is a corporation or Scottish firm, show the name on surname line and registered or principal office on the usual residential line.

Give previous forenames or surname(s) except:
- for a married woman, the name by which she was known before marriage need not be given.
- for names not used since the age of 18 or for at least 20 years

A peer or individual known by a title may state the title instead of or in addition to the forenames and surname and need not give the name by which that person was known before he or she adopted the title or succeeded to it.

Other directorships.
Give the name of every company incorporated in Great Britain of which the person concerned is a director or has been a director at any time in the past five years.

You may exclude a company which either is, or at all times during the past five years when the person concerned was a director, was
- dormant
- a parent company which wholly owned the company making the return, or
- another wholly owned subsidiary of the same parent company.

Figure 5.2 *continued*

period for appointing auditors, unless the directors have decided to deliver unaudited accounts.

Appointment is by ordinary resolution on special 28 days' notice to shareholders. Remuneration, including expenses, is fixed by the shareholders in general meeting. Auditors stay in office until the end of that meeting and continue in office unless dismissed by ordinary (majority) vote of the shareholders or new auditors are appointed.

If for any reason the company is without an auditor, the directors or the company in general meeting can appoint a temporary replacement. If one is not appointed by the meeting, the company must notify the Secretary of State within seven days of the meeting, when the Secretary of State may make the appointment.

The auditors must be members of one of the following:

- The Institute of Chartered Accountants in England and Wales;
- The Institute of Chartered Accountants of Scotland;
- The Institute of Chartered Accountants in Ireland;
- The Association of Chartered Certified Accountants;
- The Association of Authorised Public Accountants.

A director or employee cannot be the company's auditor, but the auditor can act as the company's accountant, preparing company accounts and VAT and PAYE returns and generally giving secretarial assistance and taxation advice. A limit for the financial year on the auditors' liability can be fixed by the shareholders by ordinary resolution.

Responsibility for the proper administration of company affairs, however, rests with the directors. The auditors' only responsibility is for any loss caused by their own negligence or fraud. Their reports and conclusions must be based on proper investigation and they are entitled to access to all necessary documents and information. If they are not satisfied that your books and accounts properly reflect the company's financial circumstances, this must be stated in their report.

The company seal

Article 101 of the draft model Articles requires the company to use a company seal – usually a metal disc with the name of the company on it in raised letters – as the company's 'signature' impressed on documents that have to be made by deed. These include commercial contracts, leases, share certificates, debentures and mortgages. Its use must be authorised by the directors and two directors or a director and the company secretary, if any, have to sign the document for and on behalf of the company.

Now, the signatures of the two directors or the director and company secretary, signing for and on behalf of the company, has the same effect as if the document had been executed (signed) under seal. If you do not want to use a seal, Article 101 must be cancelled.

Share issues

The directors must ensure that the Articles are complied with on share issues. The secretary records the issue of shares in the minutes of the meeting at which they are issued, and makes the appropriate entries in the Register of members to show the new shareholders' names and addresses and details of the shares issued.

Entries in the minutes and Register must also be made when shares are transferred.

Share certificates

The secretary completes share certificates, which are numbered and state the number and class of shares issued. The certificate is signed by a director and the secretary and, if required by the Articles, sealed with the company seal.

Meetings

Your private company does not have to hold Annual General Meetings or any other meeting, except to remove a director or the auditors. Most decisions can be made on written resolutions by simple or 75 per cent majority and contact with shareholders can be by post, e-mail or the company's website.

If you decide to call meetings they must be called and run in accordance with the draft model Articles. Directors' meetings can be run in any way that the directors think fit and minutes of their meetings need only be made available to the directors, the secretary, if any, and the auditors.

Procedure is more closely regulated for full company/shareholders' meetings. No business can be transacted unless a quorum of two shareholders or the single shareholder in a single shareholder company or their proxy is present within 30 minutes of the time of the meeting. Failing their attendance the meeting must be adjourned to the same time, day and place the following week, or the time and place designated by the directors.

Adequate records must be kept of decisions, whether made at meetings or by written resolution, including:

- copies of resolutions;
- minutes of proceedings;
- details of decisions, including the decisions of the sole shareholder of a sole shareholder company.

The company and officers in default are liable to fines if records are not retained for three years. They must be available for inspection by shareholders, who can request copies on payment of a minimum fee of £3.50.

Single-member companies

The single-member company must, like any other company, have at least one director and a secretary who cannot also be the sole director. The single member, present in person or by proxy, constitutes a quorum for meetings. A single-member 'shareholders' meeting' must be minuted as such and decisions must be formally notified to the company, including the contract between the company and the single shareholder.

The first board meeting

No notice is prescribed for calling board meetings. If a meeting is called, a majority of the directors must attend; a quorum of two directors is required by the draft model Articles.

The company exists from the date the Registrar issues the Certificate of Incorporation, but a great deal of important business cannot be dealt with until the first board meeting and it should therefore be held on the same day as, or as soon as possible after, incorporation.

Business will include:

- A report on the incorporation of the company. The Certificate of Incorporation should be produced.
- Reporting the appointment of the first directors and secretary.
- Appointing the chairperson.
- Appointing any additional directors.
- Reporting on the situation of the registered office and deciding whether it should be changed.
- Confirming the authorised users of the company seal and signatories OR deciding to change the draft model Articles to dispense with its use.
- Agreeing the opening of the bank account and naming the signatories, for instance any two directors or a director and the secretary. Your bank will provide a form of company mandate (agreement) which sets out the necessary wording. This must be sent to them with a copy of the Memorandum and Articles of Association and they will want to see the Certificate of Incorporation.
- The allotment of shares (other than the subscribers' shares) and a record of receipts of any payment received for the subscribers' shares and for any other shares allotted. Sealing of share certificates must be minuted.
- Appointing the auditors and deciding on the accounting reference date.

You may also want to appoint a managing director or chairperson, appoint solicitors, deal with matters relating to the company's trading activities and with general administrative matters, and disclose the directors' interests in contracts.

The meeting must be minuted by the secretary, but minutes of directors'/board meetings are not available for shareholders' inspection. They should therefore be kept in a Minute Book separate from that used for minutes of company (shareholders') meetings.

General meetings

The shareholders acting together in general meeting can do anything *intra vires* (within the powers of) the company as set out in its Articles, but in practice, control of the company is delegated to the directors and exercised by resolutions passed in general meeting.

Minutes of meetings must be kept in the Minute Book kept for that purpose and when signed by the chair of the meeting or the next successive meeting constitute evidence of the proceedings.

Voting

The draft model Articles provide that voting is by a show of hands; each member regardless of his or her shareholding then has one vote. The draft model Articles provide that the chair, or any two shareholders, or shareholders holding not less than one-tenth of the total voting rights, can demand a poll, when voting is normally on the basis of one vote per share held. Proxies (authorised by absent shareholders to vote on their behalf) are entitled to vote and special voting rights attached to shares are taken into account before deciding whether a motion has been carried.

A director's personal interest in a company contract disqualifies the director from voting; if he or she does so the transaction can be set aside.

The Annual General Meeting

Private companies do not have to hold Annual General Meetings, but it may be convenient to call a general shareholders' meeting within 18 months of incorporation and once in every subsequent calendar year, 15 months being the longest permitted interval between meetings, to:

- receive the annual accounts and the directors' report;
- propose the dividend;
- elect or dismiss directors;
- dismiss or appoint auditors and fix their remuneration.

However, you can instead circulate the information to shareholders and decisions can be made by written resolution.

The holders of at least one-twentieth of the voting shares can force the company to present a resolution at the Annual General Meeting and to send their comments about it to all the shareholders. In exceptional circumstances a single director or shareholder can ask the court to order a meeting.

Extraordinary General Meetings

Any other company business is usually 'special' and requires an Extraordinary General Meeting, with notice to shareholders of what is to be discussed. The meeting is usually convened by the secretary, on the directors' instructions, to deal with business that cannot await the next Annual General Meeting.

Subject to the Articles, two or more holders of more than one-tenth of the fully paid-up voting shares can demand that the directors call a meeting within 21 days. In default, a meeting can be called by at least half of those shareholders within three months of the request.

Notice of meetings

If you decide to hold meetings, notice of the meeting and of what is to be discussed must be sent to shareholders and the auditors in accordance with the Articles. The draft model Articles specify 14 clear days notice, excluding the day on which notice is given and the day of the meeting, unless shareholders holding at least 90 per cent of the voting shares have agreed a shorter notice period or to waive it altogether.

You must give 28 clear days' notice of a resolution to dismiss, appoint or prevent the reappointment of auditors or to remove or replace directors.

Notice by post is considered given when posted and received 48 hours after posting. It can also be given partly or wholly in hard copy or electronically or put on your website. Notice must state the time, date and place of the meeting and the general nature of business to be transacted. If sent by website it must remain on the website until the meeting has concluded. An accidental omission to give notice, or its non-receipt, will not invalidate proceedings at meetings.

Resolutions

Your private company does not have to serve notice of resolutions or call and hold meetings at all, provided resolutions can be approved by the company or any class of its shareholders by the requisite majority of shareholders entitled to vote.

Decisions can instead be made on written resolutions sent to shareholders in hard copy and/or electronically, posted on the company's website or (if it would not cause undue delay) by passing the resolution from one shareholder to another.

Resolutions must be accompanied by relevant documentation, they must state how to vote, the majority required and the date by which they must be passed; they must also be sent to the auditors.

Written resolutions cannot be used to remove directors or auditors before the end of their term of office.

Resolutions may be ordinary or special. *Ordinary resolutions* are passed by a straight majority of shareholders entitled to vote. A three-quarters majority and 28 days' special notice is required for *special resolutions* to:

- dismiss a director;
- replace a dismissed director;
- dismiss an auditor;
- appoint a new auditor.

Most private company business including the removal of directors and auditors only requires an ordinary resolution.

Special resolutions must be stated as such. They are required to:

- amend the Articles;
- reduce or re-denominate share capital;
- approve a payment out of the company's capital for redemption or purchase of its shares;
- opt in or out of automatic suspension of potential barriers to takeovers on a takeover bid;
- resolve on a voluntary winding up – unless the Articles provide that the company be wound up after a fixed time or on a specified event;
- approve the acceptance by the liquidator in a shareholders' voluntary liquidation of shares of another company to which assets of the liqiuidating company are to be transferred;
- give the liquidator in a shareholders' voluntary winding up powers to pay a class of creditors in full or make a compromise or arrangement concerning the company's debts or of a debt owed to the company;
- petition to the court for a compulsory winding up.

Copies of special resolutions and resolutions that become part of the company's constitution and affect outsiders, for instance, debtors, creditors and prospective shareholders, must be filed with the Registrar within 15 days of the meeting or decision.

Five per cent of the shareholders can at their own expense require the company to circulate a resolution, provided it is not defamatory, frivolous or vexatious, or, if passed, would be ineffective. It must be accompanied by an explanatory statement of not more than 1,000 words.The company and anyone claiming to be aggrieved by the resolution can apply for a court order to prevent its circulation.

The directors and secretary, if any, are liable to fines of up to £1,000 and a daily default fine of up to £100 if records are incomplete and/or copies are not sent to the Registrar within the time limits.

6

Changes after incorporation

Changes made after incorporation involve formalities, and some decisions can only be made by the shareholders in general meeting and necessitate filing forms and copy documents with the Registrar.

The directors are responsible for keeping the Registrar informed and there are penalties if some of the documentation is not filed.

Some of the documentation must be signed by a director and/or the company secretary and some by the chairperson of the relevant meeting. The documents you are most likely to use are discussed in this chapter and listed in Appendix 3 and draft forms of resolutions are set out in Appendix 5.

You can now file notices, copies of accounts and reports with Companies House electronically via e-mail or by posting them on the Companies House website, www.companieshouse.gov.uk.

You can also send the accounts, summary financial statements and reports electronically to shareholders, debenture-holders and the auditors or, provided you notify the recipients, publish them on your company's website for at least 14 days before the meeting until the termination of the meeting at which they are to be laid. Notices on a website must contain specified details about the meeting and the shareholders can send proxy forms and other notices to you via e-mail.

Change of directors and secretary

Directors are elected, re-elected and dismissed by the directors or a majority vote on an ordinary resolution. The shareholders do not vote on the appointment or removal of the company secretary.

Removal is by majority vote and the shareholders and the director must have 28 days' notice of the resolution. The director can make written representations which, if there is sufficient time, must accompany the resolution. If not, the director can require them to be read out at the meeting.

If there is no service contract or notice provisions in their contract, directors can resign at any time on notice.

Shareholders have to approve voluntary payments to directors for loss of office. A memorandum with details of the proposed payment must be available for inspection at the registered office for 15 days before the meeting or, if to be approved by written resolution, sent to shareholders with the resolution. Approval is not required for a total payment of £200 or a pension in respect of past services.

The shareholders must have special notice of at least 28 days of a resolution to prevent re-appointment or to remove or replace serving directors. Notice must also be given to the person concerned and to the auditors.

Directors can put their objections to removal to the shareholders or require the company to circulate their written representations. The notice of the resolution sent to shareholders must state that they have made written representations.

Changes of directors and secretary must be filed with the Registrar within 14 days of the change on Form 288b (see page 63).

Changing the auditors

Auditors are appointed at each Annual General Meeting to hold office from the conclusion of the meeting until the conclusion of the next AGM, unless the directors have decided that audited accounts are unlikely to be required.

They must be appointed during the 28 days beginning with the day the accounts and reports were sent out, or, if later, during the 28 days beginning with the end of the period for sending out copies of the accounts and reports. Remuneration, including expenses, is fixed by the shareholders.

Appointment can be made at any time before the expiry of the term of office agreed separately with the directors. They may be entitled to compensation for premature termination of the separate agreement.

They cease to hold office for the following year unless reappointed and are assumed to be reappointed unless:

- a replacement is appointed,
- auditors are appointed by the directors,

- the Articles require actual reappointment, or
- 5 per cent of the shareholders serve notice that they are not deemed to be reappointed before the end of the accounting reference period after which deemed reappointment would have taken effect.

Retiring auditors or auditors removed before the expiration of their term of office may address the meeting called to appoint a successor, or require the company to circulate their comments to shareholders. The resolution for the replacement should state that the retiring auditors have made written representations and are entitled to attend company meetings which discuss matters dealt with during their term of office.

The directors or the company in general meeting can fill casual vacancies but the appointment must be confirmed by resolution at the Annual General Meeting. Unless the court orders otherwise, a copy of the auditor's statement must be sent to the Registrar.

Special notice of 28 days is required for resolutions appointing new auditors, and to reappoint an auditor appointed to fill a casual vacancy or to remove one before expiry of his or her term of office.

Notice of removal of the auditors must be sent to the Registrar on Form 391 within 14 days of the meeting.

The auditors can be indemnified out of the company's assets against any liability incurred in defending civil or criminal proceedings in which they obtain judgment or if they are not liable for negligence, default, breach of duty or breach of trust in relation to the company's affairs.

Change of registered office

Changes must be notified to the Registrar within 14 days of the change on Form 287 (see page 109).

Changes in the place where statutory records and documents are kept

Notice of any change in the place where the statutory registers and documents are kept must be filed with the Registrar within 14 days of the change.

Companies House
— for the record —

10

First directors and secretary and intended situation of registered office

Please complete in typescript, or in bold black capitals.

CHWP000

Notes on completion appear on final page

Company Name in full

Proposed Registered Office

(PO Box numbers only, are not acceptable)

Post town

County / Region | Postcode

If the memorandum is delivered by an agent for the subscriber(s) of the memorandum mark the box opposite and give the agent's name and address.

Agent's Name

Address

Post town

County / Region | Postcode

Number of continuation sheets attached

You do not have to give any contact information in the box opposite but if you do, it will help Companies House to contact you if there is a query on the form. The contact information that you give will be visible to searchers of the public record.

Tel

DX number | DX exchange

Companies House receipt date barcode

This form is been provided free of charge by Companies House

v 08/02

When you have completed and signed the form please send it to the Registrar of Companies at:

Companies House, Crown Way, Cardiff, CF14 3UZ **DX 33050 Cardiff**
for companies registered in England and Wales

or

Companies House, 37 Castle Terrace, Edinburgh, EH1 2EB
for companies registered in Scotland **DX 235 Edinburgh**

Figure 6.1 Notice of passing of resolution removing an auditor

Company Secretary (see notes 1-5)

Company name

NAME *Style / Title *Honours etc

* Voluntary details

Forename(s)

Surname

Previous forename(s)

Previous surname(s)

Address

Usual residential address
For a corporation, give the registered or principal office address.

Post town

County / Region Postcode

Country

I consent to act as secretary of the company named on page 1

Consent signature **Date**

Directors (see notes 1-5)
Please list directors in alphabetical order

NAME *Style / Title *Honours etc

Forename(s)

Surname

Previous forename(s)

Previous surname(s)

Address

Usual residential address
For a corporation, give the registered or principal office address.

Post town

County / Region Postcode

Country

Day Month Year

Date of birth **Nationality**

Business occupation

Other directorships

I consent to act as director of the company named on page 1

Consent signature **Date**

Figure 6.1 *continued*

Directors (continued) (see notes 1-5)

NAME	*Style / Title		*Honours etc
* Voluntary details	Forename(s)		
	Surname		
	Previous forename(s)		
	Previous surname(s)		
Address			
Usual residential address For a corporation, give the registered or principal office address.			
	Post town		
	County / Region		Postcode
	Country		
		Day Month Year	
Date of birth			**Nationality**
Business occupation			
Other directorships			
		I consent to act as director of the company named on page 1	
Consent signature			**Date**

This section must be signed by
Either

an agent on behalf of all subscribers	**Signed**		**Date**
***Or* the subscribers**	**Signed**		**Date**
(i.e those who signed as members on the memorandum of association).	**Signed**		**Date**
	Signed		**Date**
	Signed		**Date**
	Signed		**Date**
	Signed		**Date**

Figure 6.1 *continued*

Change of name

The company's name is changed by a 75 per cent majority vote of the shareholders on a special resolution in general meeting or on a written resolution signed by all the shareholders. A copy of the signed resolution must be sent to the Registrar with notification of the change within 15 days of the decision or meeting, with the £10 fee for entry on the Index or £50 for a same-day change. The restrictions on choice of name are set out in Appendix 1. The change is effective from the date of issue by the Registrar of an altered Certificate of Incorporation.

Increases in capital and allotment of shares

The company's capital can be increased by ordinary resolution.

When there is only one class of shares, the directors can allot more shares of the same class or grant rights to subscribe for shares or issue securities convertible into shares without first offering them to the other shareholders, unless this is prohibited by the Articles.

If there is more than one class of shares they can only be allotted if authorised by the Articles or by ordinary shareholders' resolution. The authority must state the maximum number of shares that can be allotted. It must also state when the authorisation expires, which must not be more than five years from the date of incorporation if specified in the Articles or five years from the resolution authorising the allotment.

Authorisation can be renewed for a maximum of five years, or revoked or varied at any time by shareholders' resolution.

If the authorisation permits the company to make an offer or agreement which may require shares to be allotted after its expiration, the directors can proceed with the offer or agreement after authorisation has expired.

A copy of the relevant resolution must be sent to the Registrar within 15 days of the resolution and no capital duty is payable.

Within 2 months of the allotment a Return of Allotments form signed by a director or the secretary must be filed with the Registrar. If the shares or rights are issued or granted for cash, the form to be completed is 88(2) (see page 120); otherwise Form 88(3) (see page 35) must be filed, together with a copy of the contract of sale or details specified on the form and a statement of capital.

Companies House
— for the record —

287

Change in situation or address of Registered Office

Please complete in typescript, or in bold black capitals.
CHWP000

Company Number

Company Name in full

New situation of registered office

NOTE:

The change in the situation of the registered office does not take effect until the Registrar has registered this notice.

For 14 days beginning with the date that a change of registered office is registered, a person may validly serve any document on the company at its previous registered office.

PO Box numbers only are not acceptable.

Address

Post town

County / Region | Postcode

Signed | **Date**

† Please delete as appropriate.

† a director / secretary / administrator / administrative receiver / liquidator / receiver manager / receiver

You do not have to give any contact information in the box opposite but if you do, it will help Companies House to contact you if there is a query on the form. The contact information that you give will be visible to searchers of the public record.

Tel

DX number DX exchange

Companies House receipt date barcode

This form has been provided free of charge by Companies House.

10/03

When you have completed and signed the form please send it to the Registrar of Companies at:

Companies House, Crown Way, Cardiff, CF14 3UZ **DX 33050 Cardiff**
for companies registered in England and Wales **or**
Companies House, 37 Castle Terrace, Edinburgh, EH1 2EB **DX 235 Edinburgh**
for companies registered in Scotland **or LP - 4 Edinburgh 2**

Figure 6.2 Change in situation or address of Registered Office

Companies House
— for the record —

353

Please complete in typescript, or in bold black capitals.

CHWP000

Register of members

Company Number

Company Name in full

The register of members is kept at:

NOTE:
The register **MUST** be kept at an address in the country of incorporation.

This notice is not required where the register has, at all times since it came into existence (or in the case of a register in existence on 1 July 1948 at all times since then) been kept at the registered office.

Address

Post town

County / Region

Postcode

Signed

Date

† Please delete as appropriate.

† a director / secretary / administrator / administrative receiver / receiver manager / receiver

You do not have to give any contact information in the box opposite but if you do, it will help Companies House to contact you if there is a query on the form. The contact information that you give will be visible to searchers of the public record.

Tel

DX number DX exchange

Companies House receipt date barcode

This form has been provided free of charge by Companies House.

Form revised 10/03

When you have completed and signed the form please send it to the Registrar of Companies at:

Companies House, Crown Way, Cardiff, CF14 3UZ DX 33050 Cardiff
for companies registered in England and Wales

or

Companies House, 37 Castle Terrace, Edinburgh, EH1 2EB
for companies registered in Scotland DX 235 Edinburgh
or LP - 4 Edinburgh 2

Figure 6.3 Register of members

Companies House
— for the record —

318

Location of directors' service contracts

Please complete in typescript, or in bold black capitals.

CHFP000

Company Number

Company Name in full

Address where directors' service contracts or memoranda are available for inspection by members.

NOTE:
Directors' service contracts **MUST** be kept at an address in the country of incorporation.

This notice is not required where the relevant documents are and have always been kept at the Registered Office.

Address

Post town

County / Region

Postcode

Signed **Date**

† Please delete as appropriate.

† a director / secretary / administrator / administrative receiver / receiver manager / receiver

Please give the name, address, telephone number and, if available, a DX number and Exchange of the person Companies House should contact if there is any query.

Tel

DX number DX exchange

Companies House receipt date barcode

This form has been provided free of charge by Companies House.

Form revised July 1998

When you have completed and signed the form please send it to the Registrar of Companies at:

Companies House, Crown Way, Cardiff, CF14 3UZ **DX 33050 Cardiff**
for companies registered in England and Wales
or
Companies House, 37 Castle Terrace, Edinburgh, EH1 2EB
for companies registered in Scotland **DX 235 Edinburgh**

Figure 6.4 Location of directors' service contracts

Companies House
— for the record —

325

Location of register of directors' interests in shares etc.

Please complete in typescript, or in bold black capitals.

CHFP000

Company Number

Company Name in full

The register of directors' interests in shares and/or debentures is kept at:

NOTE:
The register **MUST** be kept at an address in the country of incorporation.

This notice is not required where the register is and has always been kept at the Registered Office.

Address

Post town

County / Region   Postcode

Signed   **Date**

† Please delete as appropriate.

† a director / secretary / administrator / administrative receiver / receiver manager / receiver

Please give the name, address, telephone number and, if available, a DX number and Exchange of the person Companies House should contact if there is any query.

Tel

DX number   DX exchange

Companies House receipt date barcode

This form has been provided free of charge by Companies House.

Form revised July 1998

When you have completed and signed the form please send it to the Registrar of Companies at:
Companies House, Crown Way, Cardiff, CF14 3UZ   DX 33050 Cardiff
for companies registered in England and Wales
or
Companies House, 37 Castle Terrace, Edinburgh, EH1 2EB
for companies registered in Scotland   **DX 235 Edinburgh**

Figure 6.5 Location of register of directors' interests in shares, etc

G

CHFP000

COMPANIES FORM No. 325a

Notice of place for inspection of a register of directors' interests in shares etc. which is kept in a non-legible form, or of any change in that place

325a

Please do not write in this margin

Pursuant to the Companies (Registers and Other Records) Regulations 1985

Note: For use only when the register is kept by computer or in some other non-legible form

Please complete legibly, preferably in black type, or bold block lettering

To the Registrar of Companies
(Address overleaf)

For official use

Company number

Name of company

* insert full name of company

*

gives notice, in accordance with regulation 3(1) of the Companies (Registers and Other Records) Regulations 1985, that the place for inspection of the register of directors' interests in shares and/or debentures which the company keeps in a non-legible form is [now] †:

† delete as appropriate

Postcode

† delete as appropriat

Signed [Director][Secretary]† Date

Presenter's name address and reference (if any) :

For official Use (02/06)
General Section

Post room

Figure 6.6 Notice of place for inspection of a register of holders of debentures which is kept in a non-legible form, or of any change in that place

Notes

The address for companies registered in England and Wales or Wales is :-

The Registrar of Companies
Companies House
Crown Way
Cardiff
CF14 3UZ

or, for companies registered in Scotland :-

The Registrar of Companies
Companies House
37 Castle Terrace
Edinburgh
EH1 2EB

Figure 6.6 *continued*

Companies House
— for the record —

190

Location of register of debenture holders

Please complete in typescript, or in bold black capitals.
CHWP000

Company Number

Company Name in full

gives notice that †[a register][registers]†[in duplicate form] of holders of debentures of the company of the classes mentioned below †[is][are]kept at:

NOTE:
This notice is not required where the register is, and has always been, kept at the Registered Office

Address

Post town

County / region Postcode

Brief description of class of debentures

Signed **Date**

† Please delete as appropriate.

† a director / secretary

You do not have to give any contact information in the box opposite but if you do, it will help Companies House to contact you if there is a query on the form. The contact information that you give will be visible to searchers of the public record.

Tel

DX number DX exchange

Companies House receipt date barcode

This form has been provided free of charge by Companies House.

Form revised 10/03

When you have completed and signed the form please send it to the Registrar of Companies at:
Companies House, Crown Way, Cardiff, CF14 3UZ DX 33050 Cardiff
for companies registered in England and Wales
or
Companies House, 37 Castle Terrace, Edinburgh, EH1 2EB
for companies registered in Scotland DX 235 Edinburgh
or LP - 4 Edinburgh 2

Figure 6.7 Location of register of debenture holders

G

CHWP000

COMPANIES FORM No. 190a

Notice of place for inspection of a register of holders of debentures which is kept in a non-legible form, or of any change in that place

190a

Please do not write in this margin

Pursuant to the Companies (Registers and Other Records) Regulations 1985

Note: For use only when the register is kept by computer or in some other non-legible form

Please complete legibly, preferably in black type, or bold block lettering

To the Registrar of Companies
(Address overleaf)

For official use

Company number

Name of company

* insert full name of company

*

gives notice, in accordance with regulation 5(1) of the Companies (Registers and Other Records) Regulations 1985, that the place for inspection of the register of debenture holders which the company keeps in a non-legible form is [now]:

Postcode

Signed [Director][Secretary]† Date

† delete as appropriate

Presenter's name address and reference (if any) :

For official Use (02/06)
General Section

Post room

Figure 6.8 Notice of place for inspection of a register of holders of debentures which is kept in a non-legible form, or of any change in that place

Notes

The address for companies registered in England and Wales or Wales is :-

The Registrar of Companies
Companies House
Crown Way
Cardiff
CF14 3UZ
DX 33050 Cardiff

or, for companies registered in Scotland :-

The Registrar of Companies
Companies House
37 Castle Terrace
Edinburgh
EH1 2EB

DX 235 Edinburgh
or LP - 4 Edinburgh 2

Figure 6.8 *continued*

G

COMPANIES FORM No. 123

Notice of increase in nominal capital

123

CHWP000

Please do not write in this margin

Pursuant to section 123 of the Companies Act 1985

Please complete legibly, preferably in black type, or bold block lettering

To the Registrar of Companies
(Address overleaf)

For official use

Company number

Name of company

* insert full name of company

*

gives notice in accordance with section 123 of the above Act that by resolution of the company

dated ______________________ the nominal capital of the company has been

increased by £ ______________ beyond the registered capital of £ ______________.

† the copy must be printed or in some other form approved by the registrar

A copy of the resolution authorising the increase is attached. †

The conditions (eg. voting rights, dividend rights, winding-up rights etc.) subject to which the new shares have been or are to be issued are as follows :

Please tick here if continued overleaf

‡ Insert Director, Secretary, Administrator, Administrative Receiver or Receiver (Scotland) as appropriate

Signed   Designation ‡   Date

Presenter's name address and reference (if any) :

For official Use (02/06)
General Section

Post room

Figure 6.9 Notice of increase in nominal capital

Notes

The address for companies registered in England and Wales or Wales is :-

The Registrar of Companies
Companies House
Crown Way
Cardiff
CF14 3UZ

DX 33050 Cardiff

or, for companies registered in Scotland :-

The Registrar of Companies
Companies House
37 Castle Terrace
Edinburgh
EH1 2EB

DX 235 Edinburgh or LP - 4 Edinburgh 2

Figure 6.9 *continued*

Companies House
— for the record —

Please complete in typescript, or in bold black capitals.
CHWP000

88(2)

(Revised 2005)
Return of Allotment of Shares

Company Number	
Company name in full	

Shares allotted (including bonus shares):
(see Guidance Booklet GBA6)

	From			To		
	Day	Month	Year	Day	Month	Year
Date or period during which shares were allotted (If shares were allotted on one date enter that date in the "from" box)						

Class of shares (ordinary or preference etc)			
Number allotted			
Nominal value of each share			
Amount (if any) paid or due on each share (including any share premium)			

List the names and addresses of the allottees and the number and class of shares allotted to each overleaf

If the allotted shares (including bonus shares) are fully or partly paid up otherwise than in cash please state:

% that each share is to be treated as paid up			
% (if any) that each share is to be paid up in cash			

Consideration for which the shares were allotted (This information must be supported by the original or a certified copy of the contract or by Form 88(3) if the contract is not in writing)	

Companies House receipt date barcode

This form has been provided free of charge by Companies House.

09/2005

When you have completed and signed the form please send it to the Registrar of Companies at:

Companies House, Crown Way, Cardiff, CF14 3UZ for companies registered in England and Wales — DX 33050 Cardiff

or

Companies House, 37 Castle Terrace, Edinburgh, EH1 2EB for companies registered in Scotland — DX 235 Edinburgh or LP - 4 Edinburgh 2

Figure 6.10 Return of allotment of shares

Names and addresses of the allottees

Shareholder details (list joint allottees as one shareholder)	**Shares and share class allotted**	
Name(s) / Address / UK Postcode	Class of shares allotted	Number allotted
Name(s) / Address / UK Postcode	Class of shares allotted	Number allotted
Name(s) / Address / UK Postcode	Class of shares allotted	Number allotted
Name(s) / Address / UK Postcode	Class of shares allotted	Number allotted
Name(s) / Address / UK Postcode	Class of shares allotted	Number allotted

Please enter the number of continuation sheets (if any) attached to this form

Signed ______________________ **Date** ______________________

** A director / secretary / administrator / administrative receiver / receiver / official receiver / receiver manager / voluntary arrangement supervisor

** *Please delete as appropriate*

Contact Details
You do not have to give any contact information in the box opposite but if you do, it will help Companies House to contact you if there is a query on the form. The contact information that you give will be visible to searchers of the public record.

Tel
DX number DX exchange

Figure 6.10 *continued*

Companies House
— for the record —

6

Cancellation of alteration to the objects of a company

Please complete in typescript, or in bold black capitals.
CHFP000

Company Number

Company Name in full

An application was made to the Court on:

Day Month Year

for the cancellation of the alteration made to the objects of the company by a special resolution passed on:

Day Month Year

Signed **Date**

† Please delete as appropriate.

† a director / secretary / administrator / administrative receiver / receiver manager / receiver

Please give the name, address, telephone number and, if available, a DX number and Exchange of the person Companies House should contact if there is any query.

Tel

DX number DX exchange

Companies House receipt date barcode

This form has been provided free of charge by Companies House.

Form revised July 1998

When you have completed and signed the form please send it to the Registrar of Companies at:
Companies House, Crown Way, Cardiff, CF14 3UZ DX 33050 Cardiff
for companies registered in England and Wales
or
Companies House, 37 Castle Terrace, Edinburgh, EH1 2EB
for companies registered in Scotland **DX 235 Edinburgh**

Figure 6.11 Cancellation of alteration to the objects of a company

It is a criminal offence to allot shares unless authorised by the Articles or a shareholders' resolution for which the company and its officers are liable to fines of up to £1,000 plus a daily default fine of £100.

The directors do not, however require authorisation to allot shares in pursuance of an employees' share scheme, nor must they first offer those shares to other shareholders.

The draft model Articles make no provision for variation of class rights. If the new issue varies the rights of existing shareholders the variation must be approved by a three-quarters majority of that class of shareholders, and when the rights have been varied 15 per cent of those shareholders can apply to the court to have the variation cancelled. You should therefore take expert advice before acting.

Changes in the Articles of Association

Alterations in the Articles are by a majority vote of the shareholders on a special resolution. Printed and signed copies of resolutions altering the Articles must be sent to the Registrar within 15 days of the resolution, but the alteration is not effective until the Registrar has advertised it in the *Gazette*.

Changing the accounting reference date

You can change the ARD by shortening or extending (to a maximum of 18 months) the accounting period (which fixes your accounting year). You can shorten the period as often and by as many months as you like. You cannot extend the period to more than 18 months from the start date and cannot extend it more than once in five years unless:

- the company is in adminstration;
- the Secretary of State has so directed; or
- the company is aligning its ARD with a subsidiary or parent undertaking in the EC.

The change must be made during a current period and details must be sent to the Registrar on Form 225. No time limit is specified but it must be sent before the deadline for filing the accounts.

Filing the accounts

Accounts must usually be filed 10 months after the ARD. If the company's first accounts cover a period of more than 12 months, however, they must be filed within 22 months of the date of incorporation. If the accounting reference period has been shortened, the time allowed is 10 months or, if longer, three months from the date on Form 225.

For filing purposes a month after a specified date ends on the same date in the appropriate month, ie if the ARD is 30 October 2008, accounts must be filed before midnight on 30 August 2009. If there is no such date, eg the ARD ends on 30 February, accounts must be filed on the last day of the following February.

Extending the filing date

You can apply for a three-month extension:

- If you carry on business or have interests abroad. Form 244 must be delivered to Companies House before the normal filing deadline and be filed for every year the company claims the extension.
- In special circumstances, eg if something beyond the company or the auditors' control delays the accounts. Written application must be made before the filing deadline, setting out the reasons for and the length of the required extension, to the Secretary of State for Trade and Industry. Companies incorporated in England and Wales apply c/o Companies Administration Section, Companies House, Cardiff. For Scottish companies the application is to Companies House, Edinburgh.

The *annual return*. Companies House will send you 'shuttle' Annual Return Form 363s for your second and following years. The company's capital and shareholders are pre-printed on the form, which is sent with a covering letter stating when the return must be filed and what information, if any, is required to complete the return. It must be made up to the 'return date' and list changes in:

- the registered office address;
- the address at which the register of shareholders and register of debenture holders, if any, are kept;
- the company's principal business activities;
- the addresses of the directors and secretary, if any;
- the date on which any company officer has resigned.

A copy of the annual return signed by a director or the secretary, if any, must be sent to the Registrar with the registration fee of £30, or £15 if filed electronically, within 28 days of the return date.

Striking the company off the Register

Failure to file returns or accounts may lead to an enquiry as to whether the company has ceased trading and the Registrar may delete the company from the Register if:

- up-to-date information about the company's activities has not been filed; or
- there are no effective officers; or
- mail sent to the registered office is returned undelivered; or
- information is received that the company has ceased trading.

Before taking action the Registrar writes to the company to make enquiries. Failing a response, he then informs the company, and publishes notice in the *Gazette*, of his intention to strike the company off after three months unless cause is shown to the contrary. Before striking off, the Registrar considers the objections of creditors and may delay taking action in order to allow them to pursue their claims and to petition to wind up the company. Notice of striking off will then be published in the *Gazette*. If there are assets they are *bona vacantia*, that is, they belong to the Crown, the Duchy of Lancaster or the Duchy of Cornwall, depending on the location of the registered office.

7

Insolvency

Limited liability means that if the business is insolvent, management's only liability is for fraud and for recklessness and incompetence which has jeopardised the interests of the creditors.

This chapter summarises the various procedures for winding up the company, but if drastic decisions must be made you should take expert advice. All the procedures require reference to, and action by, an insolvency practitioner, who must be a member of a recognised professional body such as the Institute of Chartered Accountants or the Law Society, or authorised by the Secretary of State. The procedures involve formalities, meetings of shareholders and creditors, time limits, reporting to and filing documentation with the Registrar, and publicity. There are fines and penalties if you do not comply with the statutory requirements.

What is insolvency?

A company is legally insolvent if it is unable to pay its debts and discharge its liabilities as and when they fall due, or the value of its assets is less than its liabilities. In determining liabilities, contingent and prospective liabilities must be taken into account, as well as actual and quantified amounts. Day-to-day involvement in management often gives a false picture of the company's financial position. If customers are slow to pay, plant, machinery and stock have been purchased under credit agreements and the company's bank account is in overdraft, the business may be far from healthy, however heavy the order book. Financial problems need not, however, lead to liquidation. The procedures introduced by the 1986 Insolvency Act permit a company to reach a compromise agreement with creditors, or to apply to the court for an administration order, so that company affairs can be reorganised and supervised, and insolvency avoided.

You should therefore ensure that you have adequate accounting records and proper financial advice so that you are able to consider taking appropriate action.

Voluntary striking off

If a company has effectively ceased to operate, the Registrar may consider a written request to strike the company off the Register. If the company is struck off, any remaining assets pass to the Crown, the Duchy of Lancaster or the Duchy of Cornwall, depending on the location of the registered office. If there are debts, the creditors can object and, in any event, the directors', management's and shareholders' liability continues as if the company had not been dissolved.

Voluntary arrangements: compositions and schemes of arrangement

Arrangements with creditors

These procedures offer a relatively straightforward method whereby a potentially solvent company concludes a legally effective arrangement with creditors with minimum reference to the court.

Procedure

The directors, or the liquidator or administrator (see below), put a statement of affairs – which sets out the company's financial position – and detailed proposals to creditors and shareholders for a scheme or composition in satisfaction of debts. They must nominate an insolvency practitioner to supervise the arrangement and, unless he or she is a liquidator or administrator, he or she must report to the court as to the necessity for shareholders' and creditors' meetings and notify creditors. A liquidator or administrator must call meetings but need not report to court. The meetings must approve the supervisor and can accept, modify or reject the proposals. Secured and preferred creditors are protected;

directors, shareholders, creditors and the supervisor can challenge decisions and implementation.

The arrangement is carried out by the supervisor, who must report to the court, which can stay (stop) the winding up and discharge an administration order. It does not need the court's approval.

Administration orders

This procedure is mainly for companies which do not borrow on standard fixed and floating charges. It enables a potentially or actually insolvent company to put its affairs in the hands of an administrator, so that part or all of the company can be salvaged or a more advantageous realisation of assets can be secured than on a winding up.

Application is made to the court, which must be satisfied that the company is, or is likely to become, unable to pay its debts. In addition, the court must consider:

- that the order would be likely to enable part or all of the undertaking to survive as a going concern;
- and/or creditors are likely to agree a satisfactory arrangement with the company;
- and/or realisation of the assets is likely to be more advantageous than if the company were wound up.

The order can be used together with a voluntary arrangement or compromise or arrangement with creditors under the Companies Acts but not if the company is already in liquidation.

The petition is presented to the court by the company and/or directors and/or creditors and notice must be given to debenture-holders who have appointed, or have the right to appoint, an administrative receiver under a floating charge. On presentation of the petition, the administrator takes over management and no legal proceedings can issue or continue against the company, but an administrative receiver can be appointed and a petition for winding up can be presented. A more detailed statement of affairs verifed on affidavit by current and former officers of the company and, in some circumstances, employees, is drawn up. The administrator's proposals for reorganisation, which depend on the terms of the court order, can be rejected by shareholders, creditors or the court, although the creditors' approval is not mandatory.

Receivership

This is the procedure by which assets secured by a floating charge are realised. Secured creditors can enforce their security independently of a winding up and without regard to the unsecured creditors or to the interests of the company.

Administrative receivers are appointed under a debenture secured by a charge and the appointment can be over all or a substantial part of the company's assets. The appointment can be by the debenture-holders or the court, and again the administrative receiver takes over management.

Receivers are appointed under the terms of a fixed charge or by the court but they cannot act as administrative receivers. Their powers depend on the terms of the charge or court order. The appointment suspends the fixed charge holders' right to enforce their security without the consent of the court or administrator, who can dispose of the charged property, giving them the same priority as they would have had if they had enforced the charge directly.

Receivers and directors

The directors' powers effectively cease when a receiver or administrative receiver is appointed. A receiver ceases to act when he or she has sufficient funds to discharge the debt due to his or her appointor and his or her expenses, but an administrative receiver can only be removed by court order.

Voluntary arrangement

There have been frequent complaints that secured creditors, particularly banks, act primarily in their own interests and ignore the interests of other creditors and the company.

With some exceptions appointing an administrative receiver has been barred under charges created on or after 20 June 2003. Instead, securities must be enforced through the appointment of an administrator who owes a duty to and has to account to all the company's creditors.

The appointment can still be made by the court, but holders of a floating charge can on two days' notice, or the company or its directors on five days' notice, choose instead to file a notice of appointment with the court. No reports have to be filed explaining why the company should go into administration. However, the company or the directors (but not the floating charge-holder) must file a statement that the company is or is likely to become unable to pay its debts, and that the administrator believes that the purpose of administration is reasonably likely to be achieved.

The administrator then takes over management of the company to:

- rescue the company as a going concern; or
- achieve a better result for the creditors as a whole than would be likely if the company were wound up without first going into administration; or
- realise the assets in order to make a distribution to the secured or preferential creditors.

There is an overall time limit of one year for the process of administration, with an extension of six months with the creditors' consent or longer if the court so orders. If the administrator is unable to rescue the company, he or she must file a notice with the court converting to a creditors' voluntary liquidation and he or she acts as liquidator unless the creditors decide otherwise.

Protection for floating charge-holders

The floating charge-holder can choose his or her own administrator even if there is already an application before the court, unless the court decides otherwise, and can also apply for the appointment of an administrator if the company is in compulsory liquidation.

Voluntary arrangement with a moratorium

This scheme requires proposals for a voluntary arrangement being put to the company by a nominated insolvency practitioner, who calls shareholders' and creditors' meetings to approve the voluntary arrangement and on approval supervises the arrangement. When the proposals are drawn up and supported by the nominee the directors can obtain a 28-day moratorium (which stops creditors and others from enforcing their legal remedies) by filing the terms of the proposals and certain other documents with the court. There must be both creditors' and shareholders' meetings, the moratorium must be advertised and the registrar notified. The 28-day period can be shortened and, with the creditors' consent, extended by two months.

During the moratorium the nominee monitors the company's affairs and the directors cannot act without his or her consent. The moratorium ends with the calling of the required meetings that either approve or reject the voluntary arrangement. If there is disagreement, the decision of the creditors' meeting is decisive.

Winding up

This is the statutory procedure which brings a company's operations to an end. Business letters, order forms and company websites must state that the company is being wound up. Company assets are realised and the proceeds distributed among creditors and shareholders in accordance with their rights, and the company is dissolved.

A company can be wound up compulsorily by court order or voluntarily by the shareholders if it is insolvent, or by shareholders if it is solvent.

In a shareholders' voluntary winding up directors, shadow directors, and their 'connections' must give shareholders details of transactions in which they acquire, or will acquire, directly or indirectly, a substantial non-cash asset (see page 67) from the company, and of transactions in which the company acquires or is to acquire a substantial non-cash asset from them. Failing full disclosure and shareholder approval the transaction may be set aside and the directors, shadow directors and their 'connections' may have to account to the company for any profits. Shareholder approval is not required if the company is in administration or being compulsorily wound up.

Voluntary winding up

The company puts itself into voluntary liquidation by passing a resolution at a general meeting of the shareholders. Seven days' notice of the meeting must be given and a notice of a creditors' meeting to be held on the same day or the day after must be sent on the same date. The decision can be by ordinary resolution if the company was formed for a fixed period or a specific undertaking; otherwise a special resolution must be passed. An extraordinary resolution is necessary if the company is insolvent.

Voluntary liquidation

A members' or shareholders' voluntary liquidation requires the majority of the directors to prepare a declaration of solvency after full enquiry into the company's affairs. The declaration sets out the company's assets and liabilities and states that it will be able to pay its debts within, at most, 12 months; if they are not paid, the directors may be liable to a fine or imprisonment.

If no declaration is made or the liquidator disagrees with its conclusion or the company cannot pay its debts within 12 months, it becomes a creditors' voluntary liquidation and the creditors appoint and can supervise the liquidator.

The advantage of a voluntary liquidation is that, although employees are dismissed if the company is insolvent, the directors can continue to act provided they have the approval of the liquidator and of the shareholders given in general meeting. In a creditors' voluntary liquidation the creditors must also give their consent.

If the resolution is passed without appointing a liquidator, the directors can dispose of perishable goods and those likely to diminish in value unless immediately disposed of, and take action necessary to protect company assets until one is appointed. Any further action requires the consent of the court, and the company must stop trading except in so far as may be required for beneficial winding up.

The liquidation starts on the date the resolution for winding up is passed; if the liquidator thinks the company is insolvent, the winding up continues as a creditors' voluntary liquidation. The liquidator stays in office until removed after his or her final report to shareholders and creditors but he or she can resign or vacate office on notice to the Registrar of the final meeting.

Distribution

Available assets are applied against the company's liabilities, and shareholders are only called on for any balance remaining unpaid on their shares.

Subject to creditors' rights and with the approval of a shareholders' special resolution a private company's liquidator can distribute all or part of the company's assets between the shareholders *in specie* – without converting them into cash. The liquidator can value the assets and decide how to divide them between the shareholders or vest all or part of them on trust for the shareholders' benefit. The shareholders are not compelled to accept assets burdened with debt or other liabilities.

Creditors' rights

Fixed charge-holders take the first slice of the assets, followed by liquidation expenses, preferential debts, floating chargeholders and sums due to shareholders (for instance, arrears of dividend). In some circumstances floating chargeholders may have prior claims to holders of a fixed charge. Remaining assets go to unsecured creditors, who can claim interest to the date of distribution, and any surplus is divided among shareholders in accordance with their rights under the Memorandum and Articles of Association.

Preferential debts comprise:

- outstanding tax to a maximum of 12 months, including PAYE;
- contributions in respect of subcontractors in the construction industry;
- six months' VAT;
- general betting duty;
- 12 months' National Insurance contributions;
- state and occupational pension scheme contributions;
- arrears of wages for four months (including directors but not the managing director) to a maximum of £240 per week, including Statutory Sick Pay, protective awards, payment during medical suspension, time off work and accrued holiday pay.

Wages Act employee claims are paid if the company has more than 10 employees. Most amounts payable to employees under the employment legislation can be reimbursed partly or wholly from the Redundancy Fund. Employees can claim for any balance still outstanding with the ordinary (unsecured) creditors.

Claims in tort – such as claims in damages for negligence – are provable debts in liquidation or administration proceedings. There must be *prima facie* evidence of the claim at the date the company went into liquidation or entered administration. Quantification of the compensation claimed is not required.

Dissolution in a voluntary liquidation

The company is dissolved three months from registration by the Registrar of the liquidator's final account and return.

Compulsory winding up

The compulsory procedure can be initiated by the company, a shareholder, a creditor, the official receiver (employed by the Insolvency Service), or the Department for Business, Enterprise and Regulatory Reform.

The most frequent basis for the petition is insolvency, which here is presumed if a creditor has been owed at least £750 for more than three weeks after a formal demand has been served, or the company has not discharged a judgment debt or court order. The court appoints a liquidator who can, without reference to the court or creditors, take over management of the company forthwith. Here the liquidator not only gets in and distributes the assets but also must provide the official receiver with any information and documents he or she requires. The official receiver must look into the cause of the company's failure, reporting if necessary to the court, and he or she can apply for public examination of officers, liquidators, administrators and anyone else involved in the company's affairs.

Fines and penalties

If the company has been trading with an intent to defraud creditors or anyone else, or incurring debts without a reasonable prospect of repayment, anyone involved may be prosecuted and disqualified from participating directly or indirectly in the management of a company for a maximum of 15 years. Conviction for an indictable offence (that is, a serious offence triable by jury in the Crown Court) relating to the promotion, formation, management or liquidation of a company, or with the receivership or management of its property, or for persistent failure to file accounts and records, can also lead to disqualification.

Fraudulent and wrongful trading can in addition bring a personal liability for all the company's debts. Fraudulent trading is trading with an intent to defraud creditors. If the company is in insolvent liquidation and a director, *de facto*, or shadow director knew, or should have known, that there was no reasonable prospect that the company could have avoided insolvent liquidation, there may also be criminal liability for wrongful trading and disqualification.

Officers of the company and anyone else acting in the promotion, formation, management or liquidation of a company in liquidation are personally liable if they retain or misapply assets or they are in breach of duty to the company.

Voidable transactions: preferences and transactions at an undervalue

Any transaction entered into by an insolvent company which puts a creditor, surety or guarantor into a better position than he or she would be in the liquidation may be voidable and set aside as a (fraudulent) 'preference'. The preference may be a transaction at a proper price or at an undervalue (that is, a gratuitous gift or transfer or one made for significantly less than market value). The risk period dates back from presentation of a petition for an administrative order or the date the order is made, or the commencement of liquidation.

Transactions at a proper price or an undervalue are safe if made in good faith and for the purpose of carrying on the business, provided that at the time there were reasonable grounds for believing that the transaction would benefit the company. They are at risk, however, if made at a time when the company was unable to pay its debts or it became unable to pay them as a result of the transaction. Preferences at an undervalue and any preference, even one at a proper price, with a connected person is at risk for two years. There is a six-month risk period for other preferences and preferences made in the period prior to the making of an administration order.

The network of connected persons here extends further and includes:

- directors;
- shadow directors, ie persons in accordance with whose instructions directors are accustomed to act;
- company officers and their spouses, including former and reputed spouses;
- their children and step-children;
- their partners;
- companies with which they are associated;
- companies of which they control at least one-fifth of the voting shares;
- trustees of any trust under which they, their family group or an associated company is a beneficiary.

Floating charges may also be voidable. They are valid whenever created to the extent that consideration (that is, payment in cash, goods or services or in discharge of debts) is received by the company. The balance is at risk for one year if made when the company was unable to pay its debts, and two years if made in favour of a connected person.

Distribution is on the same basis as in voluntary liquidation.

Dissolution in compulsory winding up

The liquidator reports to a final meeting of creditors when winding up is completed. If the official receiver is acting, he or she can apply for early dissolution on the basis that assets will not cover winding up expenses and no further investigation is required. Three months from the date of registration of dissolution entered by the Registrar, the company is dissolved.

Restriction on use of the company name

Directors and shadow directors acting within 12 months of insolvent liquidation cannot act for, or be involved with, a company with the same name. Nor can they for five years use a former name or trading name used during the previous 12 months or one so similar as to suggest continuing association, without the consent of the court. Non-compliance brings a personal joint and several liability with the company and anyone acting on the offender's instructions.

8

The ready-made company

The fastest way to incorporation is to buy an 'off the shelf', ready-made company already registered at Companies House from your solicitor or accountant or one of the many registration agents who advertise in financial and professional journals and the *Yellow Pages*. All the necessary documentation will have been filed with the Registrar and the company will have a Certificate of Incorporation, so that it can start trading as soon as you have appointed your own director(s) and secretary and transferred the shares to your own shareholders.

Your solicitor or accountant can incorporate your company through a company agent's fast-track electronic filing service for under £25 plus VAT. If you want to choose your own company name they will check its availability for a fee. If you intend to use the name as a trade mark, you should also carry out a search at the Trade Marks Registry in the appropriate class of goods and services.

Companies House will send you information packs and guides, and agents will advise you on the necessary initial changes for takeover. The objects clause can be changed but you should ensure that the existing principal objects clause covers your main business activities.

You will then have a company with a current Certificate of Incorporation, a standard Memorandum of Association with an appropriate objects and capital clause, standard Articles of Association, a set of statutory books and a company seal if this is required by your Articles. The existing directors, secretary and shareholders of the ready-made company, usually the agent's nominees, resign in favour of your nominees.

If the nominee shareholders were companies, your ready-made company cannot claim exemption from audit for its accounts (see page 90), unless it is dormant throughout its first financial year. It may therefore be worthwhile shortening the first accounting period so it ends on the day on which you take ownership of the shares. The company must, however, pass a special resolution not to appoint auditors and deliver dormant company accounts for the first (shortened) period, before the first general meeting at which accounts are laid.

You may wish to make other changes, which must be notified to the Registrar of Companies in accordance with the Companies Act, and which are dealt with in Chapter 6. These involve some delay, but the procedure is more straightforward and less expensive than starting from scratch.

Appendix 1

Notes for guidance on company names

A. Use of the following words and expressions or thier plural or possessive forms in a company name requires the prior approval of the Secretary of State for Business, Enterprise and Regulatory Reform.

(a) *Words that imply national or international pre-eminence*

International
National
European
United Kingdom
Great Britain
British
England
English
Scotland
Scottish
Wales
Welsh
Ireland
Irish

(b) *Words that imply business pre-eminence or representative or authoritative status*

Association
Council
Institution
Authority
Federation
Society
Board
Institute

(c) *Words that imply specific objects or functions*

Assurance
Assurer
Benevolent
Charter
Chartered
Chemist
Chemistry
Co-operative
Foundation
Friendly society
Fund
Group
Holding
Industrial & Provident Society
Insurance
Insurer
Patent
Patentee
Post office
Re-assurance
Re-assurer
Register
Registered
Re-insurance
Re-insurer
Sheffield
Stock exchange
Trade union
Trust

B. Use of the following words and expressions also requires the prior consent of the relevant body as well as the Secretary of State. A statement that a written request has been made to the relevant body seeking its opinion as to use of the word or expression must be filed with the application for registration, together with a copy of any response:

Word or expression	*Relevant body for persons intending to to set up business in England or Wales*	*Relevant body for persons intending to set up business Scotland*
Charity, Charitable	Head of Status Charity Commission Woodfield House Tangier Taunton TA1 4BL	Inland Revenue FICO (Scotland) Trinity Park House South Trinity Road Edinburgh EH5 3SD
Royal, Royale, Royalty King, Queen, Prince Princess, Windsor, Duke, His/Her Majesty	Linda Henshawe Ministry of Justice Constitutional Settlement Division 6th Floor Point 6B Selbourne House 54 Victoria Street London SW1E 6QW (if based in England) The National Assembly for Wales Crown Buildings Cathays Park Cardiff CF1 3NQ (if based in Wales)	Douglas Boyd Protocol Unit St Andrew's House Regent Road Edinburgh EG1 3DG

Police	Pauline Laybourne Briefing & Honours Team CRCSG Change & Support Unit 3rd Floor A Fry Building 2 Marsham Street London SW1P 4DF	The Scottish Ministers Police Division St Andrew's House Regent Road Edinburgh EG1 3DG
Special School	Department for Education and Skills Caxton House 6–12 Tothill Street London SW1 H 9NA	As for England and Wales
Contact Lens	General Optical Council 41 Wimpole Street, London W1N 2DJ	As for England and Wales
District Nurse, Health Visitor, Midwife, Midwifery, Health Visiting, Nurse, Nursing	The Registrar and Chief Executive United Kingdom Central Council for Nursing and Midwifery 23 Portland Place London W1N 3AF	As for England and Wales
Health Centre	Office of the Solicitor Department of Health and Social Security 48 Carey Street London WC2A 2LS	As for England and Wales
Health Service	Penny Turner Head of Branding Room 230B Shipton House 80 London Road London SE1 6LH	As for England and Wales

Pregnancy, Termination, Abortion	Department of Health Area 423 Wellington House 133–5 Waterloo Road London SE1 8UG	As for England and Wales
Dental, Dentistry	The Registrar General Dental Council 37 Wimpole Street London W1M 8DQ	As for England and Wales
Polytechnic	Department of Education and Science FHE1B Sanctuary Buildings Great Smith Street London SW1P 3BT	As for England and Wales
University	Privy Council Office 2 Carlton Gardens London SW1Y 5AA	As for England and Wales

C. The use of the following words or expressions is covered by other legislation and may constitute a criminal offence. If you wish to use them, you should contact the relevant regulatory authority or ask Companies House for advice before proceeding. Companies House may seek independent advice from the relevant body.

Word or expression	*Relevant legislation*	*Relevant body*
Architect	Section 20 Architects Registration Registration Act 1997	Architects Registration Board 73 Hallan Street London W1N 6EE
Building Society	Building Society Act 1986	Seek advice of Companies House

Chiropodist, Dietician, Medical Laboratory, Technician, Occupational Therapist, Orthoptist, Physiotherapist, Radiographer, Remedial Gymnast,	Professions supplementary to Medicine Act 1960 if preceded by Registered, State or State Registered	Mrs Jan Arnott Department of Health Room 2N35A HRD HRB Quarry House Quarry Hill Leeds LS2 7JE
Credit Union	Credit Union Act 1979	The Public Records Section Financial Services Authority 25 North Colonnade Canary Wharf London E14 5HS Scottish Association Associate Registrar of Friendly Societies 58 Frederick Street Edinburgh EH2 1NB
Dentist, Dental Surgeon, Dental Practitioner, Dentistry	Dental Act 1984	The Registrar General Dental Council 37 Wimpole Street London W1M 8DQ
Druggist, Pharmaceutical, Pharmaceutist, Pharmacist, Pharmacy	Section 7B Medicines Act 1968	Director of Legal Services Royal Pharmaceutical Society of Great Britain 1 Lambeth High Street London SE1 7JN

		For Scotland Pharmaceutical Society 36 York Place Edinburgh EH1 3HU
Optician, Ophthalmic Optician, Dispensing Optician, Enrolled Optician, Registered Optician, Optometrist	Opticians Act 1989	The Registrar General Optical Council 41 Harley Street London W1N 2DJ
Solicitor (Scotland)	Act of Scotland 1980	The Law Society of Scotland 26 Drumsheugh Gardens Edinburgh EH3 7HR
Veterinary Surgeon, Veterinary, Vet	Sections 19/20 Veterinary Surgeons Act 1966	The Registrar Royal College of Veterinary Surgeons Belgravia House 62–64 Horseferry Road London SW1P 2AF
Red Cross, Geneva Cross, Red Crescent, Red Lion and Sun	Geneva Convention Act 1957	Seek advice of Companies House
Anzac	Anzac Act 1916	Seek advice of Companies House
Inst of Laryngology, Inst of Otology, Inst of Urology, Inst of Orthopaedics	University College of London Act 1988	Seek advice of University College Gower Street London WC1E 6BT

Olympiad, Olympiads, Olympian, Olympians, Olympic, Olympics, Paralympic, Paralympics, Paralympiad, Paralympiads, Paralympian, Paralympians, translations of these or similar words	Use may infringe rights of British Olympic Association/British Paralympic Association	Games Ltd 23rd Floor 1 Churchill Place Canary Wharf London E14 5LN

Also protects Olympic symbols of 5 interlocking rings and Olympic and Paralympic mottos.

The London Olympic and Paralympic Games Act 2006 further protects Olympic words, symbols and marks relating to the Games; registration of a company name which includes words implying association with the Games may infringe the rights of the London Organising Committee. Further information available at www.london2012.com/brand/protection.

Patent Office, Patent Agent	Copyright Design & Patents Act 1988	IPDD, Room 3B38 Concept House The Patent Office Cardiff Road Newport NP10 8QQ
Building Society and Friendly Society	Building Society Act 1986 Friendly Society Act 1874	The Registry of Friendly Societies 25 The North Colonnade Canary Wharf London E14 5HS

Chamber(s) of Business, Chamber(s) of Commerce, Chamber(s) of Commerce & Industry, Chamber(s) of Commerce, Training & Enterprise, Chamber(s) of Enterprise, Chamber(s) of Industry, Chamber(s) of Trade, Chamber(s) of Trade and Industry, Chamber(s) of Training, Chamber(s) of Training and Enterprise or Welsh translations of these words	Company & Business Names (Chamber of Commerce etc) Act 1999	Guidance available from Companies House

Bank, banker, banking or deposit do not need approval BUT using words suggesting banking activities implies you are carrying on a banking business and accept deposits. This is a regulated activity under the Financial Services and Markets Act 2000 and may constitute an offence unless you are an 'authorised person' or have exemption under the Act.

Only persons carrying on business as a building society in the United Kingdom may use a name that implies that they are in any way connected with the business of a building society.

D. 'Too like' names – The Secretary of State takes account of facts which might suggest similarity and lead to confusion, including, for instance, the nature and location of a business. Evidence to show confusion is taken into account.

E. A name suggesting a connection with a company already on the Index – The Secretary of State does not consider 'implied association' – ie whether the company might be thought to be a member of, or associated with, another company or group. Nor is consideration given to trading names, logos, trade or service marks, copyrights, patents, etc or any other proprietary rights existing in names or parts of names.

F. Company letterhead – Business owned by a company:

Bert's Shoes

6 Tuppeny Passage, London NW12 5TT

Bert's Shoes (UK) Limited
Registered in England and Wales
Registration Number: 123456789
Registered Office, 81 Florin Way, London NW13 7DD

The restrictions applying to business names are similar to those applying to company names.

Information required to be disclosed by the Business Names Act 1985 and the Companies Act 1985.

Appendix 2

Documents to be filed on incorporation by a private limited company

1. An application for registration of the company;
2. A statement of capital and initial shareholdings;
3. A statement of proposed officers (Form 10);
4. A statement of compliance with the Requirements on Application for Registration of a Company (Form 12).

SCHEDULE 1 — Regulation 2(a)

COMPANY HAVING A SHARE CAPITAL

Memorandum of association of [*insert name of company*]

We, the subscribers to this memorandum of association, wish to form a company under the Companies Act 2006 and agree to become members of the company and to take at least one share each.

Names of subscribers	*Authentication by subscribers*

Dated

Figure A2.1 Memorandum of association

Appendix 3

Documents which must be lodged with the Registrar*

Document	*Form*	*Signatories*	*When lodged*
Statement of first directors secretary and intended situation of registered office	10	Subscribers or their agent and each officer	Before registration
Declaration of compliance with requirements on application for registration	12	Director, secretary or solicitor acting	ditto
Notice of change of registered office	287	Director or secretary	Within 14 days of change

* The documentation listed covers the more straightforward company business. It does not include documentation which must be filed when you are involved in transactions requiring specialist legal and/or accountancy advice.

Notice of change of directors, secretary or in their particulars	288	ditto	ditto
Document	*Form*	*Signatories*	*When lodged*
Contract constituting allottees' title to shares and contract of sale	–	All parties to contract	Within 14 days of change
Particulars of contract re shares allotted as fully or partly paid up otherwise than in cash	88(3)	Director or secretary	Within 1 month of allotment of shares for non-cash consideration (used when no written contract)
Return of allotment of shares	88(2)	ditto	Within 1 month of allotment
(first) Notice of accounting reference date	224	ditto	Within 9 months of incorporation
Notice of new accounting reference date	225	ditto	Before end of period
Accounts	225	Director	Within 10 months of accounting reference period

Annual return	363a	Director or secretary	Within 28 days of the return date
Special resolution	–	Director, secretary or chairman of meeting	Within 15 days of passing resolution
Extraordinary resolution	–	Director, secretary or chairman of meeting	Within 15 days of passing resolution
Other resolution or agreement by all members or class of members not otherwise effective unless passed as special or extraordinary resolution	–	ditto	ditto
Resolution authorising increase of share capital	–	ditto	ditto
Notice of increase in nominal capital	123	Director or secretary	ditto
Notice of passing of resolution removing an auditor	386	ditto	Within 14 days of passing resolution
Notice of place where copies of director's service contracts kept or of change in place	318	ditto	Within 14 days

Notice of place where register of members kept or of change in place	353	ditto	ditto
Notice of place where register of holders of debentures or duplicate kept or of change in place	190	ditto	Not specified
Notice of place where register of directors' interests in shares, etc, kept or of change in place	325	Director or secretary	Within 14 days daily
Particulars of mortgage or charge	395	Director, secretary, solicitor to company or mortgagee	Within 21 days of creation (instrument also to be produced)
Particulars for registration of charge to secure series of debentures	397	Director, secretary, solicitor to company or debenture holder or their solicitor	Within 21 days of execution of trust deed or debentures (if no deed) and the deed or one debenture
Particulars of a mortgage or charge subject to which property has been acquired	400	Director or secretary	Within 21 days of acquisition

Declaration of satisfaction in full or in part of mortgage or charge	403a	Under company seal at company's option but best attested as required by articles	lodged forthwith
Declaration that part of property or undertaking (a) has been released from charge; (b) no longer forms part of undertaking	403b	Under company seal attested as required by articles	At company's option but best lodged forthwith
Notice of appointment receiver or manager	405(1)*	Person obtaining order or making appointment or their solicitor	Within 7 days of court order or appointment
Notice of ceasing to act as receiver or manager	405(2)*	Receiver or manager	On ceasing to act
Printed copy of memorandum as altered by special resolution	–	–	Within 15 days after period for making application to court for cancelling alteration

*Not illustrated

Note: Companies House prefers forms to be completed online, printed, dated, signed and posted. Directions are available on their website.

Typed and handwritten documents must be completed legibly in black ink or black type on white A4 paper with a matt finish or of a background density not greater than

0.3 and with a margin of not less than 10 mm on each side. Letters and numbers must be at least 1.8 mm high, with a density of at least 1.0. Computer print is acceptable but dot matrix and carbon is not.

There is no charge for viewing some company documents online, others can be viewed for £1–£4 and single documents can be viewed or downloaded for £1.

The charge for a paper copy ordered by post or telephone and sent by post or fax is £3.

Companies House also provides bulk compilations, including company analysis listed by VAT trade classification, postcode, incorporation date or company status and a Register of Directors, Register of Registered Charges and New Incorporation Prints. More detailed analysis of the information held by Companies House is available on request.

High-volume users, for instance company formation agents, can use the electronic incorporation service but otherwise filing is by post, Document Exchange or courier. Faxed copies of statutory documents are not accepted for registration. Acknowledgement of receipt of documents is only given if postage or carriage is pre-paid.

Enquiries can be made by e-mail to enquiries@companieshouse.gov.uk and by telephone to 0870 333 3636 or fax to 02920 380517.

G

COMPANIES FORM No. 128(1)

Statement of rights attached to allotted shares

128(1)

CHW P000

Please do not write in this margin

Pursuant to section 128(1) of the Companies Act 1985

Please complete legibly, preferably in black type, or bold block lettering

To the Registrar of Companies
(Address overleaf)

For official use

Company number

Name of company

* insert full name of company

*

has allotted shares with rights which:

i. are not stated in the company's memorandum or articles or in any resolution or agreement to which section 380 of the above Act applies, and

ii. are not in all respects uniform with those attached to shares previously allotted.

† delete as appropriate

The class[es]† of such shares and the date of the first allotment of shares in each class and the rights attached to each class are:

Class of Shares	Date of first allotment
Description of Rights	

‡ Insert Director, Secretary, Administrator, Administrative Receiver or Receiver (Scotland) as appropriate

Signed Designation‡ Date

Presenter's name address and reference (if any) :

For official Use (02/06)
General Section
Post room

Figure A3.1 Statement of rights attached to allotted shares

G

CHW P000

COMPANIES FORM No. 128(3)

Statement of particulars of variation of rights attached to shares

128(3)

Please do not write in this margin

Pursuant to section 128(3) of the Companies Act 1985

Please complete legibly, preferably in black type, or bold block lettering

To the Registrar of Companies
(Address overleaf)

For official use

Company number

Name of company

* insert full name of company

*

† insert date

On † ______________________ the rights attached to

Number of Shares	Class(es) of share

were varied as set out below (otherwise than by amendment of the company's memorandum or articles or by any resolution or agreement to which section 380 of the above Act applies)

‡ Insert Director, Secretary, Administrator, Administrative Receiver or Receiver (Scotland) as appropriate

Signed Designation‡ Date

Presenter's name address and reference (if any) :

For official Use (02/06)
General Section
Post room

Figure A3.2 Statement of particulars of variation of rights attached to shares

Notes

The address for companies registered in England and Wales or Wales is :-

The Registrar of Companies
Companies House
Crown Way
Cardiff
CF14 3UZ

or, for companies registered in Scotland :-

The Registrar of Companies
Companies House
37 Castle Terrace
Edinburgh
EH1 2EB

Figure A3.2 *continued*

G

CHW P000

COMPANIES FORM No. 128(4)

Notice of assignment of name or new name to any class of shares

128(4)

Please do not write in this margin

Pursuant to section 128(4) of the Companies Act 1985

Please complete legibly, preferably in black type, or bold block lettering

To the Registrar of Companies
(Address overleaf)

For official use

Company number

Name of company

* insert full name of company

*

† delete as appropriate

gives notice of the assignment of a [new]† name or other designation to the following class[es]† of shares (otherwise than by amendment of the company's memorandum or articles or by any resolution or agreement to which section 380 of the above Act applies)

Number and class of shares	Name or other designation

‡ Insert Director, Secretary, Administrator, Administrative Receiver or Receiver (Scotland) as appropriate

Signed Designation‡ Date

Presenter's name address and reference (if any) :

For official Use (02/06)
General Section
Post room

Figure A3.3 Notice of assignment of name or new name to any class of shares

Notes

The address for companies registered in England and Wales or Wales is :-

The Registrar of Companies
Companies House
Crown Way
Cardiff
CF14 3UZ

or, for companies registered in Scotland :-

The Registrar of Companies
Companies House
37 Castle Terrace
Edinburgh
EH1 2EB

Figure A3.3 *continued*

G

CHWP000

Please do not write in this margin

COMPANIES FORM No. 155(6)(a)

Declaration in relation to assistance for the acquisition of shares

155(6)a

Pursuant to section 155(6) of the Companies Act 1985

Please complete legibly, preferably in black type, or bold block lettering

To the Registrar of Companies
(Address overleaf - Note 5)

For official use

Company number

Name of company

Note
Please read the notes on page 3 before completing this form.

* insert full name of company

*

Ø insert name(s) and address(es) of all the directors

I/We ø

† delete as appropriate

§ delete whichever is inappropriate

[the sole director][all the directors]† of the above company do solemnly and sincerely declare that:

The business of the company is:

(a) that of a [recognised bank][licensed institution]† within the meaning of the Banking Act 1979§

(b) that of a person authorised under section 3 or 4 of the Insurance Companies Act 1982 to carry on insurance business in the United Kingdom§

(c) something other than the above§

The company is proposing to give financial assistance in connection with the acquisition of shares in the [company] [company's holding company

Limited]†

The assistance is for the purpose of [that acquisition][reducing or discharging a liability incurred for the purpose of that acquisition].†

The number and class of the shares acquired or to be acquired is:

Presenter's name address and reference (if any) :

For official Use (02/06)
General Section

Post room

Page 1

Figure A3.4 Declaration in relation to assistance for the acquisition of shares

The assistance is to be given to: (note 2) ______________________

____

____

____

Please do not write in this margin

Please complete legibly, preferably in black type, or bold block lettering

The assistance will take the form of:

The person who [has acquired][will acquire]† the share is:

† delete as appropriate

____

____

The principal terms on which the assistance will be given are:

The amount of cash to be transferred to the person assisted is £ ______________________

The value of any asset to be transferred to the person assisted is £ ______________________

The date on which the assistance is to be given is ______________________

Page 2

Figure A3.4 *continued*

Please do not write in this margin

Please complete legibly, preferably in black type, or bold block lettering

I/We have formed the opinion, as regards the company's initial situation immediately following the date on which the assistance is proposed to be given, that there will be no ground on which it could then be found to be unable to pay its debts. (note 3)

* delete either (a) or (b) as appropriate

(a) [I/We have formed the opinion that the company will be able to pay its debts as they fall due during the year immediately following that date]* (note 3)

(b) [It is intended to commence the winding-up of the company within 12 months of that date, and I/we have formed the opinion that the company will be able to pay its debts in full within 12 months of the commencement of the winding up.]* (note 3)

And I/we make this solemn declaration conscientiously believing the same to be true and by virtue of the provisions of the Statutory Declarations Act 1835.

Declared at ______________________ Declarants to sign below

____

____

on Day Month Year

before me ______________________

A Commissioner for Oaths or Notary Public or Justice of the Peace or a Solicitor having the powers conferred on a Commissioner for Oaths.

NOTES

1 For the meaning of "a person incurring a liability" and "reducing or discharging a liability" see section 152(3) of the Companies Act 1985.

2 Insert full name(s) and address(es) of the person(s) to whom assistance is to be given; if a recipient is a company the registered office address should be shown.

3 Contingent and prospective liabilities of the company are to be taken into account - see section 156(3) of the Companies Act 1985.

4 The auditors report required by section 156(4) of the Companies Act 1985 must be annexed to this form.

5 The address for companies registered in England and Wales or Wales is:-

The Registrar of Companies
Companies House
Crown Way
Cardiff
CF14 3UZ

DX 33050 Cardiff

or, for companies registered in Scotland:-

The Registrar of Companies
37 Castle Terrace
Edinburgh
EH1 2EB

DX 235 Edinburgh

or LP-4 Edinburgh 2

Page 3

Figure A3.4 *continued*

G

CHWP000

COMPANIES FORM No. 169

Return by a company purchasing its own shares

169

Please do not write in this margin

Pursuant to section 169 of the Companies Act 1985

Please do not write in the space below. For Inland Revenue use only.

Please complete legibly, preferably in black type, or bold block lettering

To the Registrar of Companies
(Address overleaf)

For official use

Company number

Name of company

* insert full name of company

*

Note
This return must be delivered to the Registrar within a period of 28 days beginning with the first date on which shares to which it relates were delivered to the company

Shares were purchased by the company under section 162 of the above Act as follows:

§ A private company is not required to give this information

Class of shares			
Number of shares purchased			
Nominal value of each share			
Date(s) on which the shares were delivered to the company			
Maximum prices paid § for each share			
Minimum prices paid § for each share			

The aggregate amount paid by the company for the shares to which this return relates was:	£
Stamp Duty is payable on the aggregate amount at the rate of $^1/_2$% rounded up to the nearest multiple of £5	£

‡ Insert Director, Secretary, Administrator, Administrative Receiver or Receiver (Scotland) as appropriate

Signed Designation ‡ Date

Presenter's name address and reference (if any) :

For official Use (02/06)
General Section

Post room

Figure A3.5 Return by a company purchasing its own shares

1. Before this form is delivered to Companies House it must be "stamped" by the Inland Revenue Stamp Office to confirm that the appropriate amount of Stamp Duty has been paid. The Inland Revenue Stamp Offices is located at:

   London Stamp Office
   Ground Floor
   South West Wing
   Bush House
   Strand
   London
   WC2B 4QN

   Tel: 020 7438 7252/7452

   Cheques for Stamp Duty must be made payable to "Inland Revenue - Stamp Duties" and crossed "Not Transferable".

   NOTE. This form must be presented to the Inland Revenue Stamp Office for stamping together with the payment of duty within 30 days of the purchase of the shares, otherwise Inland Revenue penalties may be incurred.

2. After this form has been "stamped" and returned to you by the Inland Revenue it must be sent to:

   For companies registered in:

   England or Wales:

   The Registrar of Companies
   Companies House
   Crown Way
   Cardiff CF14 3UZ

   DX: 33050 Cardiff

   Scotland:

   The Registrar of Companies
   Companies House
   37 Castle Terrace
   Edinburgh EH1 2EB

   DX: 235 Edinburgh

   or LP - 4 Edinburgh 2

Figure A3.5 *continued*

G

CHWP000

COMPANIES FORM No. 173

Declaration in relation to the redemption or purchase of shares out of capital

173

Please do not write in this margin

Pursuant to section 173 of the Companies Act 1985

Please complete legibly, preferably in black type, or bold block lettering

To the Registrar of Companies
(Address overleaf - Note 4)

For official use | Company number

Name of company

* insert full name of company

*

Note
Please read the notes on page 2 before completing this form.

ø insert name(s) and address(es) of all the directors

I / We ø ______________________________

† delete as appropriate

[the sole director][all the directors]† of the above company do solemnly and sincerely declare that:

The business of the company is:

§ delete whichever is inappropriate

(a) that of a [recognised bank][licensed institution]† within the meaning of the Banking Act 1979§

(b) that of a person authorised under section 3 or 4 of the Insurance Companies Act 1982 to carry on insurance business in the United Kingdom§

(c) that of something other than the above§

The company is proposing to make a payment out of capital for the redemption or purchase of its own shares

The amount of the permissible capital payment for the shares in question is £____________ (note 1)

Continued overleaf

Presenter's name address and reference (if any) :

For official Use (02/06)
General Section | Post room

Figure A3.6 Declaration of satisfaction in full or in part of mortgage or charge

I / We have made full enquiry into the affairs and prospects of the company, and I / we have formed the opinion:

(a) as regards its initial situation immediately following the date on which the payment out of capital is proposed to be made, that there will be no grounds on which the company could then be found unable to pay its debts (note 2), and

(b) as regards its prospects for the year immediately following that date, that, having regard to my/our intentions with respect to the management of the company's business during that year and to the amount and character of the financial resources which will in my / our view be available during that year, the company will be able to continue to carry on business as a going concern (and will accordingly be able to pay its debts as they fall due) throughout that year. (note 2)

Please do not write in this margin

Please complete legibly, preferably in black type, or bold block lettering

And I / we make this solemn declaration conscientiously believing the same to be true and by virtue of the provisions of the Statutory Declarations Act 1835.

Declared at ______________________________ Declarant(s) to sign below

____

____

	Day	Month	Year
on			

before me ______________________________

A Commissioner for Oaths, or Notary Public, or Justice of the Peace, or Solicitor having the powers conferred on a Commissioner for Oaths.

Notes

1 'Permissible capital payment' means an amount which, taken together with
(i) any available profits of the company; and
(ii) the proceeds of any fresh issue of shares made for the purposes of the redemption or purchase;
Is equal to the price of redemption or purchase.
'Available profits' means the company's profits which are available for distribution (within the meaning of section 172 and 263 of the Companies Act 1985).
The question whether the company has any profits so available and the amount of any such profits is to be determined in accordance with section 172 of the Companies Act 1985.

2 Contingent and prospective liabilities of the company must be taken into account, see sections 173(4) & 517 of the Companies Act 1985.

3 A copy of this declaration together with a copy of the auditors report required by section 173 of the Companies Act 1985, must be delivered to the Registrar of Companies not later than the day on which the company publishes the notice required by section 175(1) of the Companies Act 1985, or first publishes or gives the notice required by section 175(2), whichever is the earlier.

4 The address for companies registered in England and Wales or Wales is:-

The Registrar of Companies
Companies House
Crown Way
Cardiff
CF14 3UZ

DX 33050 Cardiff

or, for companies registered in Scotland:-

The Registrar of Companies
Companies House
37 Castle Terrace
Edinburgh
EH1 2EB

DX 235 Edinburgh
or LP-4 Edinburgh 2

Page 2

Figure A3.6 *continued*

Companies House
— for the record —

Please complete in typescript, or in bold black capitals.
CHWP000

190

Location of register of debenture holders

Company Number

Company Name in full

gives notice that †[a register][registers]†[in duplicate form] of holders of debentures of the company of the classes mentioned below †[is][are]kept at:

NOTE:
This notice is not required where the register is, and has always been, kept at the Registered Office

Address

Post town

County / region

Postcode

Brief description of class of debentures

Signed

Date

† Please delete as appropriate.

† a director / secretary

You do not have to give any contact information in the box opposite but if you do, it will help Companies House to contact you if there is a query on the form. The contact information that you give will be visible to searchers of the public record.

Tel

DX number

DX exchange

Companies House receipt date barcode

This form has been provided free of charge by Companies House.

Form revised 10/03

When you have completed and signed the form please send it to the Registrar of Companies at:
Companies House, Crown Way, Cardiff, CF14 3UZ DX 33050 Cardiff
for companies registered in England and Wales
or
Companies House, 37 Castle Terrace, Edinburgh, EH1 2EB
for companies registered in Scotland DX 235 Edinburgh
or LP - 4 Edinburgh 2

Figure A3.7 Notice of a place where a register of holders of debentures or a duplicate is kept or of any change in that place

Companies House
— for the record —

Please complete in typescript, or in bold black capitals.

CHFP000

325

Location of register of directors' interests in shares etc.

Company Number

Company Name in full

The register of directors' interests in shares and/or debentures is kept at:

NOTE:
The register **MUST** be kept at an address in the country of incorporation.

This notice is not required where the register is and has always been kept at the Registered Office.

Address

Post town

County / Region Postcode

Signed **Date**

† Please delete as appropriate.

† a director / secretary / administrator / administrative receiver / receiver manager / receiver

Please give the name, address, telephone number and, if available, a DX number and Exchange of the person Companies House should contact if there is any query.

Tel

DX number DX exchange

Companies House receipt date barcode

This form has been provided free of charge by Companies House.

Form revised July 1998

When you have completed and signed the form please send it to the Registrar of Companies at:
Companies House, Crown Way, Cardiff, CF14 3UZ DX 33050 Cardiff
for companies registered in England and Wales
or
Companies House, 37 Castle Terrace, Edinburgh, EH1 2EB
for companies registered in Scotland **DX 235 Edinburgh**

Figure A3.8 Location of register of directors' interests in shares, etc

G

CHFP000

COMPANIES FORM No. 325a

Notice of place for inspection of a register of directors' interests in shares etc. which is kept in a non-legible form, or of any change in that place

325a

Please do not write in this margin

Pursuant to the Companies (Registers and Other Records) Regulations 1985

Note: For use only when the register is kept by computer or in some other non-legible form

Please complete legibly, preferably in black type, or bold block lettering

To the Registrar of Companies
(Address overleaf)

For official use | Company number

Name of company

* insert full name of company

*

gives notice, in accordance with regulation 3(1) of the Companies (Registers and Other Records) Regulations 1985, that the place for inspection of the register of directors' interests in shares and/or debentures which the company keeps in a non-legible form is [now] †:

† delete as appropriate

Postcode

† delete as appropriat

Signed [Director][Secretary]† Date

Presenter's name address and reference (if any) :

For official Use (02/06)
General Section | Post room

Figure A3.9 Notice of a place for inspection of a register of directors' interests in shares, etc, which is kept in a non-legible form, or of any change in that place

Notes

The address for companies registered in England and Wales or Wales is :-

The Registrar of Companies
Companies House
Crown Way
Cardiff
CF14 3UZ

or, for companies registered in Scotland :-

The Registrar of Companies
Companies House
37 Castle Terrace
Edinburgh
EH1 2EB

Figure A3.9 *continued*

G

CHWP000

COMPANIES FORM No. 353a

Notice of place for inspection of a register of members which is kept in a non-legible form, or of any change in that place

353a

Please do not write in this margin

Pursuant to the Companies (Registers and Other Records) Regulations 1985

Note: For use only when the register is kept by computer or in some other non-legible form

Please complete legibly, preferably in black type, or bold block lettering

To the Registrar of Companies
(Address overleaf)

For official use

Company number

Name of company

* insert full name of company

*

gives notice, in accordance with regulation 3(1) of the Companies (Registers and Other Records) Regulations 1985, that the place for inspection of the register of members of the company which the company keeps in a non-legible form is [now] †:

† delete as appropriate

Postcode

Signed [Director][Secretary]† Date

Presenter's name address and reference (if any) :

For official Use (02/06)
General Section

Post room

Figure A3.10 Notice of a place for inspection of a register of members which is kept in a non-legible form, or of any change in that place

Notes

The address for companies registered in England and Wales or Wales is :-

The Registrar of Companies
Companies House
Crown Way
Cardiff
CF14 3UZ
DX 33050 Cardiff

or, for companies registered in Scotland :-

The Registrar of Companies
Companies House
37 Castle Terrace
Edinburgh
EH1 2EB

DX 235 Edinburgh
or LP - 4 Edinburgh 2

Figure A3.10 *continued*

M

CHWP000

COMPANIES FORM No. 397a

Particulars of an issue of secured debentures in a series

397a

Please do not write in this margin

Pursuant to section 397 of the Companies Act 1985

Please complete legibly, preferably in black type, or bold block lettering

To the Registrar of Companies
(Address overleaf - Note 3)

For official use

Company number

Name of company

* insert full name of Company

*

Note
Please read notes overleaf before completing this form

Date of present issue

Amount of present issue

Particulars as to commission, allowance or discount (note 2)

Signed ______________________ Date ______________

† delete as appropriate

On behalf of [company][mortgagee / chargee] †

Presenter's name address and reference (if any) :

For official Use (02/06)
Mortgage Section

Post room

Time critical reference

Figure A3.11 Particulars of an issue of secured debentures in a series

M

CHWP000

COMPANIES FORM No. 398

Certificate of registration in Scotland or Northern Ireland of a charge comprising property situate there

398

Pursuant to section 398(4) of the Companies Act 1985

Please do not write in this margin

Please complete legibly, preferably in black type, or bold block lettering

To the Registrar of Companies
(Address overleaf)

For official use

Company number

Name of company

* insert full name of company

*

I

of

* give date and parties to charge

certify that the charge *

of which a true copy is annexed to this form was presented for registration on

† delete as appropriate

in [Scotland] [Northern Ireland] †

Signed

Date

Presenter's name address and reference (if any) :

For official Use (02/06)
Mortgage Section

Post room

Figure A3.12 Certificate of registration in Scotland or Northern Ireland of a charge comprising property situated there

M

CHWP000

COMPANIES FORM No. 403a

Declaration of satisfaction in full or in part of mortgage or charge

403a

Please do not write in this margin

Pursuant to section 403(1) of the Companies Act 1985

Please complete legibly, preferably in black type, or bold block lettering

To the Registrar of Companies
(Address overleaf)

For official use

Company number

Name of company

* insert full name of company

*

I, ______

of ______

† delete as appropriate

[a director][the secretary][the administrator][the administrative receiver]† of the above company, do solemnly and sincerely declare that the debt for which the charge described below was given has been paid or satisfied in **[full][part]†**

insert a description of the instrument(s) creating or evidencing the charge, eg 'Mortgage', 'Charge', 'Debenture' etc

ø the date of registration may be confirmed from the certificate

§ insert brief details of property

Date and description of charge # ______

Date of registration ø ______

Name and address of [chargee][trustee for the debenture holders]† ______

Short particulars of property charged § ______

And I make this solemn declaration conscientiously believing the same to be true and by virtue of the provisions of the Statutory Declarations Act 1835.

Declared at ______

Declarant to sign below

Day Month Year

on

before me ______

A Commissioner for Oaths or Notary Public or Justice of the Peace or a Solicitor having the powers conferred on a Commissioner for Oaths.

Presenter's name address and reference (if any) :

For official Use (02/06)

Mortgage Section

Post room

Figure A3.13 Declaration of satisfaction in full or in part of mortgage or charge

Notes

The address of the Registrar of Companies is:-

The Registrar of Companies
Companies House
Crown Way
Cardiff
CF14 3UZ

Figure A3.13 *continued*

M

CHWP000

Please do not write in this margin

COMPANIES FORM No. 403b

Declaration that part of the property or undertaking charged (a) has been released from the charge; (b) no longer forms part of the company's property or undertaking

403b

Pursuant to section 403(1) (b) of the Companies Act 1985

Please complete legibly, preferably in black type, or bold block lettering

To the Registrar of Companies
(Address overleaf)

For official use

Company number

Name of company

* insert full name of company

*

I, ____________________

of ____________________

† delete as appropriate

[a director][the secretary][the administrator][the administrative receiver]† of the above company, do solemnly and sincerely declare that with respect to the charge described below the part of the property or undertaking described [has been released from the charge][has ceased to form part of the company's property or undertaking]†

\# insert a description of the instrument(s) creating or evidencing the charge, eg "Mortgage', 'Charge', 'Debenture' etc

Date and description of charge # ____________________

ø the date of registration may be confirmed from the certificate

Date of registration ø ____________________

Name and address of [chargee][trustee for the debenture holders]† ____________________

____

§ insert brief details of property or undertaking no longer subject to the charge

Short particulars of property or undertaking released or no longer part of the company's property or undertaking § ____________________

____

And I make this solemn declaration conscientiously believing the same to be true and by virtue of the provisions of the Statutory Declarations Act 1835.

Declared at ____________________

____

Declarant to sign below

Day Month Year

on

before me ____________________

A Commissioner for Oaths or Notary Public or Justice of the Peace or a Solicitor having the powers conferred on a Commissioner for Oaths.

Presentor's name address and reference (if any) :

For official Use (02/00)

Mortgage Section

Post room

Figure A3.14 Declaration that part of the property or undertaking charged (a) has been released from the charge; (b) no longer forms part of the company's property or undertaking

M

CHWP000

COMPANIES FORM No. 466(Scot)

Particulars of an instrument of alteration to a floating charge created by a company registered in Scotland

466

A fee of £13 is payable to Companies House in respect of each register entry for a mortgage or charge.

Please do not write in this margin

Pursuant to section 410 and 466 of the Companies Act 1985

Please complete legibly, preferably in black type, or bold block lettering

To the Registrar of Companies
(Address overleaf - Note 6)

For official use

Company number

Name of company

insert full name of company

*

Date of creation of the charge (note 1)

Description of the instrument creating or evidencing the charge or of any ancillary document which has been altered (note 1)

Names of the persons entitled to the charge

Short particulars of all the property charged

Presenter's name address and reference (if any):

For official use (02/06)

Charges Section

Post room

Page 1

Figure A3.15 Particulars of an instrument of alteration to a floating charge created by a company registered in Scotland

Names, and addresses of the persons who have executed the instrument of alteration (note 2)

Please do not write in this margin

Please complete legibly, preferably in black type, or bold block lettering

Date(s) of execution of the instrument of alteration

A statement of the provisions, if any, imposed by the instrument of alteration prohibiting or restricting the creation by the company of any fixed security or any other floating charge having, priority over, or ranking pari passu with the floating charge

Short particulars of any property released from the floating charge

The amount, if any, by which the amount secured by the floating charge has been increased

Figure A3.15 *continued*

A statement of the provisions, if any, imposed by the instrument of alteration varying or otherwise regulating the order of the ranking of the floating charge in relation to fixed securities or to other floating charges

Please do not write in this margin

Please complete legibly, preferably in black type, or bold block lettering

Page 3

Figure A3.15 *continued*

Continuation of the statement of the provisions, if any, imposed by the instrument of alteration varying or otherwise regulating the order of the ranking of the floating charge in relation to fixed securities or to other floating charges

Please do not write in this margin

Please complete legibly, preferably in black type, or bold block lettering

A fee is payable to Companies House in respect of each register entry for a mortgage or charge. (See Note 5)

Signed ______________________ Date ______________________

On behalf of [company] [chargee]†

† delete as appropriate

Notes

1. A description of the instrument e.g. "Instrument of Charge" "Debenture" etc as the case may be, should be given. For the date of creation of a charge see section 410(5) of the Companies Act.
2. In accordance with section 466(1) the instrument of alteration should be executed by the company, the holder of the charge and the holder of any other charge (including a fixed security) which would be adversely affected by the alteration.
3. A certified copy of the instrument of alteration, together with this form with the prescribed particulars correctly completed must be delivered to the Registrar of Companies within 21 days after the date of execution of that instrument.
4. A certified copy must be signed by or on behalf of the person giving the certification and where this is a body corporate it must be signed by an officer of that body.
5. A fee of £13 is payable to Companies House in respect of each register entry for a mortgage or charge. Cheques and Postal Orders are to be made payable to **Companies House.**
6. The address of the Registrar of Companies is: Companies Registration Office, 37 Castle Terrace, Edinburgh EH1 2EB DX 235 Edinburgh or LP - 4 Edinburgh 2

Page 4

Figure A3.15 *continued*

M

CHWP000

COMPANIES FORM No. 419a(Scot)

Application for registration of a memorandum of satisfaction in full or in part of a registered charge

419a

Please do not write in this margin

Pursuant to section 419(1) (a) of the Companies Act 1985

Please complete legibly, preferably in black type, or bold block lettering

To the Registrar of Companies
(Address overleaf)

For official use

Company number

Name of company

** insert full name of company*

*

I, ______

of ______

[a director] [the secretary] [the liquidator] [the receiver] [the administrator]† of the company, do solemnly and sincerely declare that the debt for which the charge described overleaf was given has been paid or satisfied in **[full] [part]**†

† delete as appropriate

And I make this solemn declaration conscientiously believing the same to be true and by virtue of the provisions of the Statutory Declarations Act 1835.

Declared at ______

Declarant sign below

on Day Month Year

before me ______

A Commissioner for Oaths or Notary Public or Justice of the Peace or Solicitor having the powers conferred on a Commissioner for Oaths

Presenter's name address and reference (if any):

For official use (02/06)

Charges Section

Post room

Page 1

Figure A3.16 Application for registration of a memorandum of satisfaction in full or in part of a registered charge

Particulars of the charge to which the application overleaf refers

Please do not write in this margin

Please complete legibly, preferably in black type, or bold block lettering

Date of creation of the charge

Description of the instrument (if any) creating or evidencing the charge #

 # insert a description of the instruments creating or evidencing the charge eg 'Charge', 'Debenture' etc

Date of Registration *

** the date of registration may be confirmed from the certificate*

Short particulars of property charged

Where a FLOATING CHARGE is being satisfied, the following Certificate MUST be completed:

CERTIFICATE

I ____________________

of ____________________

being [the creditor] [a person authorised to act on behalf of the creditor]† entitled to the benefits of the floating charge specified above certify that the particulars above relating to the charge and its satisfaction are correct.

† delete as appropriate

Signature ____________________ Date ____________________

Note

The address of the Registrar of Companies is:-

Companies House
37 Castle Terrace
Edinburgh
EH1 2EB

DX 235 Edinburgh
or LP - 4 Edinburgh 2

Page 2

Figure A3.16 *continued*

M

CHWP000

COMPANIES FORM No. 419b(Scot)

Application for registration of a memorandum of fact that part of the property charged (a) has been released from the charge; (b) no longer forms part of the company's property

419b

Please do not write in this margin

Pursuant to section 419(1) (b) of the Companies Act 1985

Please complete legibly, preferably in black type, or bold block lettering

To the Registrar of Companies
(Address overleaf)

For official use

Company number

Name of company

** insert full name of company*

*

I, ____________________________

of ____________________________

† delete as appropriate

[a director] [the secretary] [the liquidator] [the receiver] [the administrator]† of the company, do solemnly and sincerely declare that the particulars overleaf relating to the charge and the fact that part of the property or undertaking charged [ceased to form part of the company's property or undertaking] [was released from the charge]† on ____________________________ are true to the best of my knowledge and belief.

And I make this solemn declaration conscientiously believing the same to be true and by virtue of the provisions of the Statutory Declarations Act 1835.

Declared at ____________________________

Declarant sign below

on Day Month Year

before me ____________________________

A Commissioner for Oaths or Notary Public or Justice of the Peace or Solicitor having the powers conferred on a Commissioner for Oaths

Presenter's name address and reference (if any):

For official use (02/06)

Charges Section	Post room

Page 1

Figure A3.17 Application for registration of a memorandum of fact that part of the property charged (a) has been released from the charge; (b) no longer forms part of the company's property

Particulars of the charge to which the application overleaf refers

Please do not write in this margin

Please complete legibly, preferably in black type, or bold block lettering

Date of creation of the charge

Description of the instrument (if any) creating or evidencing the charge #

 # insert a description of the instruments creating or evidencing the charge eg 'Charge', 'Debenture' etc

Date of Registration *

** the date of registration may be confirmed from the certificate*

Short particulars of property charged

Where a FLOATING CHARGE is being satisfied, the following Certificate MUST be completed:

CERTIFICATE

I ______________________________

of ______________________________

being [the creditor] [a person authorised to act on behalf of the creditor]† entitled to the benefits of the floating charge specified above certify that the particulars above relating to the charge and the release of part of the property charged are correct.

† delete as appropriate

Signature ______________________ Date ______________

Note

The address of the Registrar of Companies is:-

Companies House
37 Castle Terrace
Edinburgh
EH1 2EB

DX 235 Edinburgh
or LP - 4 Edinburgh 2

Page 2

Figure A3.17 *continued*

Appendix 4

Books, registers and documents which must be available for inspection and of which copies or extracts can be requisitioned

Book etc	*Who can inspect*	*Fee*	*Who can requisition*	*Time limit for sending*
Memorandum and Articles	–	–	Any member	Not specified
Annual Accounts, ie auditors' report, on directors' report, balance sheet and profit and loss account	Copy to all members, debenture holders	None	Members and debenture holders	10 months or within 22 months of incorporation if period covered more than 12 months
*Accounting records	Officers at all times	None	–	–

*To be kept at the registered office or at such other place as the directors designate.

Book etc	*Who can inspect*	*Fee*	*Who can requisition*	*Time limit for sending*
Book, vouchers accounts	Auditors at all times	None	–	–
	Liquidator	–	–	–
**Charge requiring registration, copy of instrument	Members and creditors	None	–	–
Directors' service contracts, copies, or notes of their contents	Members	None	–	–
**Minute book general meeting	Members	None	Members	–
**Register of charges	Members, creditors,	None	–	–
	Anyone else	Not exceeding 5p		
*Register of debenture holders	Members, debenture holders	None	Anyone	–
	Anyone else	Not exceeding 5p		
*Register of directors and secretaries	Members	None	–	–
	Anyone else	Not exceeding 5p		

**To be kept at the registered office.

Book etc	*Who can inspect*	*Fee*	*Who can requisition*	*Time limit for sending*
**Register of directors' interests	Members Anyone else	None Not exceeding 5p	Anyone	10 days
**Register of members and index	Members Anyone else	None Not exceeding 5p	Members anyone else	Within 10 days of day after receipt of request
Special resolution	–	–	Members	Not specified
Extraordinary resolution	–	–	ditto	ditto
Members' resolution	–	–	ditto	ditto
Resolution for winding up	–	–	ditto	ditto
Trust deed securing debenture	–	–	Debenture holders	ditto

Notes:

1. Penalties: Both the company and its officers can be liable for fines.
2. Accounting records: Officers in default have a defence if they acted honestly and the default was excusable in the circumstances, but the records must be retained for at least three years.
3. Books, vouchers and accounts: If records are inadequate or access is denied, this must be stated in the auditors' report.
4. Charges requiring registration. Directors' and shadow directors' service contracts exceeding two years, the Register of Charges, Register of Debenture Holders, if any, Register of Directors and Register of Secretaries, if any, must be available for inspection.

Appendix 5

Useful notices and notes

XYZ Limited

Notice is hereby given that the First **Annual General Meeting** of the Company will be held on____day the____day of___20__ at__o'clock in the fore/after noon to transact the following business:

To receive and adopt the Accounts of the Company for the year ended____ together with the Reports of the Directors and the Auditors.

To declare a dividend.

To re-appoint/appoint________as Auditors of the Company.

To fix the remuneration of the Auditors and to transact any other business which may lawfully be transacted at an Annual General Meeting.

A member entitled to attend and vote at the above meeting may appoint a proxy to attend and vote in his stead. A proxy need not be a member of the company.

By order of the Board

Signed__________

Secretary

Figure A5.1 Notice of Annual General Meeting

Company number ____________________

Company name ____________________

We, the undersigned, being all the members of the above Company for the time being entitled to receive notice of, attend and vote at General Meetings, hereby unanimously pass the following resolution and agree that the said resolution shall pass for all purposes be as valid and effective as if the same had been passed at a General Meeting of the Company duly convened and held at:

It is resolved that:

Dated this_______day of ______ 20___

Signed: ____________________

____

____

____

Figure A5.2 Written resolution

AGREEMENT of MEMBERS to SHORT NOTICE of a GENERAL MEETING and/or of a SPECIAL RESOLUTION

(1) 'I' or 'WE'.
(2) 'Annual' or 'Extraordinary' as the case may be.

(1) ______the undersigned, being member of the above-named Company and entitled to attend and vote (2)
General Meeting of the said Company convened by a Notice of Meeting dated the day of 20 and to be held on the day of 20 , hereby agree that:

1.* The said meeting shall be deemed to have been duly called, notwithstanding that shorter notice than that specified in section 369 of the Companies Act 1985, or in the Company's Articles of Association, has been given therefor.
2.* The copies of the documents referred to in sections 239 and 240 of the Companies Act 1985, which were attached to or enclosed with the said Notice of Meeting, shall be deemed to have been duly sent, notwithstanding that such copies were sent less than twenty-one days before the date of the meeting.
3. The Special Resolution set out in the said Notice of Meeting may be proposed and passed as Special Resolution notwithstanding that such less than twenty-one days' notice of such meeting has been given.

NAME (in block capitals)	ADDRESS	SIGNATURE†

NOTES

- Delete this paragraph if not required.

† The documents referred to are the company's profit and loss account and balance sheet, the directors' report, the auditors' report and, where the Company has subsidiaries and section 229 applies, the Company's group accounts.

‡*(a)* In the case where agreement is required only to the holding of an Extraordinary General Meeting, and/or to the passing of Special Resolutions at an Extraordinary General Meeting, on short notice, agreement must be given by a majority in number of the members having a right to attend and vote at the meeting, being a majority together holding not less than 95 per cent in nominal value of the shares giving a right to attend and vote at the meeting, or, in the case of a company not having a share capital, together representing not less than 95 per cent of the total voting rights at the meeting of all the members.

(b) In any other case, agreement must be given by all the members entitled to attend and vote at the meeting.

(c) One form may be signed by all the members concerned, or several similar forms may be signed by one or more of them.

Figure A5.3 Agreements of members to short notice of a general meeting and/or of a special resolution

Section 369 (3) and *(4)* of the Companies Act 1985 provide as follows:

(3) Notwithstanding that a meeting is called by shorter notice than that specified in subsection (2) or in the company's articles (as the case may be), it is deemed to have been duly called if it is so agreed:

(a) in the case of a meeting called as the annual general meeting, by all the members entitled to attend and vote at it; and

(b) otherwise, by the requisite majority.

(4) The requisite majority for this purpose is a majority in number of the members having a right to attend and vote at the meeting, being a majority:

(a) together holding not less than 95 per cent in nominal value of the shares giving a right to attend and vote at the meeting; or

(b) in the case of a company not having a share capital, together representing not less than 95 per cent of the total voting rights at that meeting of all the members.

Section 378 (2) and *(3)* of the Companies Act 1985 provide as follows:

(2) A resolution is a special resolution when it has been passed by such a majority as is required for the passing of an extraordinary resolution and at a general meeting of which not less than 21 days' notice, specifying the intention to propose the resolution as a special resolution, has been duly given.

(3) If it is so agreed by a majority in number of the members having the right to attend and vote at such a meeting, being a majority:

(a) together holding not less than 95 per cent in nominal value of the shares giving that right; or

(b) in the case of a company not having a share capital, together representing not less than 95 per cent of the total voting rights at that meeting of all the members,

a resolution may be proposed and passed as a special resolution at a meeting of which less than 21 days' notice has been given.

Section 239 of the Companies Act 1985 provides as follows:

For the purposes of this Part, a company's accounts for a financial year are to be taken as comprising the following documents:

(a) the company's profit and loss account and balance sheet,

(b) the directors' report,

(c) the auditors' report, and

(d) where the company has subsidiaries and section 229 applies, the company's group accounts.

Section 240 of the Companies Act 1985 provides as follows:

(1) In the case of every company, a copy of the company's accounts for the financial year shall, not less than 21 days before the date of the meeting at which they are to be laid in accordance with the next section, be sent to each of the following persons:
   (a) every member of the company (whether or not entitled to receive notice of general meetings),
   (b) every holder of the company's debenture (whether or not so entitled), and
   (c) all persons other than members and debenture holders, being persons so entitled.

(2) In the case of a company not having a share capital, subsection (1) does not require a copy of the accounts to be sent to a member of the company who is not entitled to receive notices of general meetings of the company, or to a holder of the company's debentures who is not so entitled.

(3) Subsection (1) does not require copies of the accounts to be sent:
   (a) to a member of the company or a debenture holder, being in either case a person who is not entitled to receive notices of general meetings, and of whose address the company is unaware, or
   (b) to more than one of the joint holders of any shares or debentures none of whom are entitled to receive such notices, or
   (c) in the case of joint holders of shares or debentures some of whom are, and some not, entitled to receive such notices, to those who are not so entitled.

(4) If copies of the accounts are sent less than 21 days before the date of the meeting, they are, notwithstanding that fact, deemed to have been duly sent if it is so agreed by all the members entitled to attend and vote at the meeting.

Obligation to print certain documents

The Companies Act 1985

The European Communities Act 1972

1. The following documents are required to be printed:
   (a) Articles of Association
   (b) Altered Memorandums of Association
   (c) Altered Articles of Association

2. The Registrar of Companies is prepared to regard the printing stipulation as satisfied by the following processes:
   Letterpress, Gravure, Lithography.
   Stencil duplicating, Offset lithography, 'Office' typeset.
   Electrostatic photocopying.
   'Photostat' or similar processes properly processed and washed.
   Stencil duplicating, using wax stencils and black ink.

3. The following documents when submitted for registration must be either printed or in a form approved by the Registrar:
   (a) Ordinary Resolutions increasing the capital of any company.
   (b) Special and Extraordinary Resolutions and Agreements as specified in section 380 of the Companies Act 1985.

   The Registrar is prepared to accept for registration such copy Resolutions and Agreements if produced by a process named in paragraph 2 above or by spirit duplicator, of if typed.

4. No document will be accepted if it is illegible. Where it is considered that a document, though legible, cannot be reproduced to an adequate standard for presentation to the public in microfiche or photocopy form, the Registrar's practice is to seek the cooperation of the presentor in providing a clearer copy.

5. The Registrar's present practice is to accept copies of the Memorandum and Articles amended in accordance with the following rules:
   Where the amendment is small in extent, eg a change of name or a change in the nominal capital, a copy of the original document may be amended by rubber stamp, 'top copy' typing or in some other permanent manner (but not a manuscript amendment).
   An alteration of a few lines or a complete short paragraph may be similarly dealt with if the new version is satisfactorily permanently affixed to a copy of the original in such a way as to obscure the amended words.
   Where more substantial amendments are involved, the pages amended may be removed from a copy of the original, the amended text inserted and the pages securely collated. The inserted material must be 'printed' as defined above but need not be produced by the same process as the original.
   In all cases the alterations must be validated by the seal or an official stamp of the company.

6. Where the document is produced other than by letterpress, a certificate by the printer stating the process used must be endorsed on or accompany the document.
7. It has been found by experience that documents produced by semi-dry developed dye line (diazo) copies produced by spirit duplicating or thermo-copying do not satisfy the general conditions.

COMPANIES ACT 2006
WRITTEN SPECIAL RESOLUTION ON CHANGE OF NAME

Company number: ______________________________

Existing company name: ______________________________

The following special written resolution to change the name of the company was agreed and passed by the members.

On the __________ day of __________ 20_____

That the name of the company be changed to:

New name: ______________________________

Signed: ______________________
*Director / secretary / CIC Manager (if appropriate) / administrator / administrative receiver / receiver manager / receiver, on behalf of the company.
(*delete as appropriate)

Notes:

- Only a private company can pass a written resolution.
- A copy of the resolution must be delivered to Companies House within 15 days of it being passed.
- A fee of £10 is required to change the name (cheques made payable to "Companies House").
- Have you checked whether the name is available at www.companieshouse.gov.uk ?
- Please provide the name and address to which the certificate is to be sent.

Figure A5.4 Written special resolution on change of name

COMPANIES ACT 2006
SPECIAL RESOLUTION ON CHANGE OF NAME

Company number: ______________________________

Existing company name: ______________________________

At an Annual General Meeting* / General meeting* (*delete as appropriate) **of the members of the above named company, duly convened and held at:**

____

____

On the __________ **day of** __________ **20**_____

That the name of the company be changed to:

New name: ______________________________

Signed: ______________________________
*Director / secretary / CIC Manager (if appropriate) / administrator / administrative receiver / receiver manager / receiver, on behalf of the company.
(*delete as appropriate)

Notes:

- This form is for use by PLC's or private companies who choose to hold Annual General Meetings or general meetings for the purpose of a special resolution.
- A copy of the resolution must be delivered to Companies House within 15 days of it being passed.
- A fee of £10 is required to change the name (cheques made payable to "Companies House").
- Have you checked whether the name is available at www.companieshouse.gov.uk ?
- Please provide the name and address to which the certificate is to be sent.

Figure A5.5 Special resolution on change of name

WIDGETS Limited

I/We, ..., of ...., being a member/members of the above-named company, hereby appoint
.... of ...., or failing him .... of ...., as my/our proxy to vote in my/our name[s] and on my/our behalf at the general meeting of the company, to be held on .... 20 ...., and at any adjournment thereof.

This form is to be used in respect of the resolutions mentioned below as follows:

Resolution No. 1

*for *against

Resolution No. 2

*for *against

*Strike out whichever is not desired.

Unless otherwise instructed, the proxy may vote as he thinks fit or abstain from voting.

Signed this .... day of .... 20 ....

Figure A5.6 Proxy vote appointment

Appendix 6

Useful addresses

British Business Angels Association (BBAA)
New City Court
20 St Thomas Street
London SE1 9RS
Tel: 020 7089 2305
Website: www.bbaa.org.uk

British Chambers of Commerce (BCC)
65 Petty France
London SW1H 9EU
Tel: 020 7654 5800
Website: www.britishchambers.org.uk

British Insurance Brokers Association
BIBA House
14 Bevis Marks
London EC3A 7NT
Tel: 020 7623 9043
Website: www.britishinsurancebrokers.com

British Venture Capital Association
3 Clements Inn
London WC2A 2AZ
Tel: 020 7025 2950
Website: www.bvca.co.uk

Business Link
National Contact Centre: 0845 600 9006
Website: www.businesslink.org
(There are also numerous local Business Links)

Central Office of Information
Hercules House
Hercules Road
London SE1 7DU
Tel: 020 7928 2345
Website: coi.gov.uk

Chartered Association of Certified Accountants
29 Lincoln's Inn Fields
London WC2A 3EE
Tel: 020 7396 5800
Website: www.accaglobal.com

Chartered Institute of Arbitrators
12 Bloomsbury Square
London WC1A 2LP
Tel: 020 7421 7444
Website: www.arbritrators.org

Chartered Institute of Management Accountants
26 Chapter Street
London SW1P 4NP
Tel: 020 8849 2287
Website: www.cimaglobal.com

Companies House
The telephone number for all branches is 0870 33 33 636, and the website is www.companieshouse.gov.uk

Cardiff:
Crown Way
Maindy
Cardiff CF14 3UZ

London:
21 Bloomsbury Street
London WC1B 3XD

Birmingham:
Central Library
Chamberlain Square
Birmingham B3 3HQ

Leeds:
25 Queen Street
Leeds LS1 2TW

Manchester:
75 Mosley Street
Manchester M2 3HR

Edinburgh:
37 Castle Terrace
Edinburgh EH1 2EB

Competition Commission, The
Victoria House
Southampton Row
London WC1B 4AD
Tel: 020 7271 0100
Website: www.competition-commission.org

Confederation of British Industry (CBI)
Centre Point
New Oxford Street
London WC1A 1DU
Tel: 020 7379 7400
Website: www.cbi.org.uk

Consumer Credit Trade Association
The Wave
Shipley
Bradford BD17 7DU
Tel: 0845 257 1166

Department for Education and Skills
The Sanctuary Buildings
Great Smith Street
London SW1P 3BT
Tel: 0870 000 2288
Website: www.dfes.gov.uk

Department for Business, Enterprise and Regulatory Reform Ministerial Cor-respondence Unit
1 Victoria Street
London SW1H 0ET
Tel: 020 7215 5000
Website: www.berr.gov.uk

European Patent Office
Brussels, Munich, The Hague, Berlin and Vienna
Central tel: +49 89 2399 4636
Website: www.epo.org

Export Credits Guarantee Department
2 Exchange Tower
PO Box 2200
Harbour Exchange Square
London E14 9GS
Tel: 020 7512 7000
Website: www.ecgd.gov.uk

Finance and Leasing Association
2nd Floor, Imperial House
15–19 Kingsway
London WC2B 6UN
Tel: 020 7836 6511
Website: www.fla.org.uk

HM Revenue and Customs
Tax and VAT information and services online at www.hmrc.gov.uk, including addresses and telephone numbers of local offices.

Information Commissioner's Office
Head Office
Wycliffe House
Water Lane
Wilmslow
Cheshire SK9 5 AF
Tel: 08456 306060
Website: www.ico.gov.uk

Institute of Chartered Accountants in England and Wales
PO Box 433
Moorgate Place
London EC2P 2BJ
Tel: 020 7920 8100
Website: www.icaew.co.uk

Institute of Chartered Accountants in Ireland
87–89 Pembroke Road
Dublin 4
Republic of Ireland
Tel: 00 3531 637 7200
Website: www.iacai.ie

Institute of Chartered Accountants of Scotland
CA House
21 Haymarket Yards
Edinburgh EH12 5BH
Tel: 0131 347 0100
Website: www.icas.org.uk

Institute of Chartered Secretaries and Administrators
16 Park Crescent
London W1N 4AH
Tel: 020 7580 4741
Website: www.icsa.org.uk

Institute of Directors
116 Pall Mall
London SW1Y 5ED
Tel: 020 7839 1233
Website: www.iod.com

Institute of Management
Brooke House
24 Dam Street
Lichfield
Staffordshire WS13 6AB
Tel: 01543 266090
Website: www.ims-productivity.com

Insurance Ombudsman Bureau
The Financial Ombudsman Service
South Quay Plaza
183 Marsh Wall
London E14 9SR
Tel: 0845 080 1800
Website: www.financialombudsman.org.uk

International Chamber of Commerce
14–15 Belgrave Square
London SW1X 8PS
Tel: 020 7823 2811
Website: iccuk.net

Land Charges Registry
The Superintendent Land Charges Department
DX 8249
Plumer House
Tailyour Road
Crownhill
Plymouth PL6 5HY
Tel: 01752 635600
Website: landreg.gov.uk
(There are 24 Land Registries in England and Wales)

Law Society, The
113 Chancery Lane
London WC2A 1PL
Tel: 020 7242 1222
Website: www.lawsociety.org.uk

Learning and Skills Council
Cheylesmore House
Quinton Road
Coventry CV1 2WT
Tel: 0845 019 4170
Website: www.lsc.gov.uk

London Chamber of Commerce
33 Queen Street
London EC4R 1AD
Tel: 020 7248 4444
Website: www.londonchamber.co.uk
(Business Registry offers free advice and search facilities to members)

London Gazette, Edinburgh Gazette and Belfast Gazette
Website: www.gazettes-online.co.uk

Office of Fair Trading
Fleetbank House
2-6 Salisbury Square
London EC4Y 8JX
Tel: 020 7211 8000
Website: www.oft.gov.uk

The Office of Public Sector Information/Her Majesty's Stationery Office (HMSO)
St Crispins
Duke Street
Norwich NR3 1PD
Tel: 0870 600 5522
Website: www.opsi.gov.uk

Register of Judgments, Orders and Fines
Registry Trust Ltd
173–175 Cleveland Street
London W1T 6QR
Tel: 020 7380 0133
Website: www.registry-trust.org.uk

Trade Marks Registry and Patents Office
Concept House
Cardiff Road
Newport
Gwent NP10 8QQ
Tel: 01633 813930

Contact information for advertisers

Law Society Commercial Services
7th Floor, Fox Court
14 Gray's Inn Road
London WC1X 8HN
Tel: 080 7405 9075
E-mail: lfyb@lawsociety.org.uk
Website: www.lfyb.lawsociety.org.uk

Lloyds TSB Commercial Banking
Tel: 0800 022 4362
E-mail: www.lloydstsbbusiness.com/startingout

Loven
West Central
Runcorn Road
Lincoln LN6 3QP
Tel: 01522 801 111
E-mail: enquiries@loven.co.uk
Website: www.loven.co.uk

Patent Seekers
Suite 53
Imperial House
Imperial Park
Celtic Lakes
Newport NP10 8UH
Tel: 01633 816 601
E-mail: mail@patentseekers.com
Website: www.patentseekers.com

Smith & Williamson
25 Moorgate
London EC2R 6AY
Tel: 020 7131 4000
Website: www.smith.williamson.co.uk

UK Intellectual Property Office
Concept House
Cardiff Road
Newport NP10 8QQ
Tel: 08459 500 505
E-mail: enquiries@ipo.gov.uk
Website: www.ipo.gov.uk

Index

(*italics* indicate figures in the text)

Index of advertisers

KOGAN
PAGE